Joseph Lanzara

All the

OSCARS®

(We Care About)

1929   2022

A Concise Listing of
★ **All the Winners** ★
★ **All the Nominees** ★
In all the categories we care about

ISBN-13: 978-1505866858
ISBN-10: 1505866855

New Arts Library
Belleville, New Jersey
Printed in the United States of America

For Kathy, Rakhi, & Elaine

THE FIRST ACADEMY AWARDS®

Hosted by Douglas Fairbanks
Hollywood Roosevelt Hotel, Los Angeles
May 16

1929

Honoring films of 1927 and 1928

★ = **WINNER**
Followed by   OTHER NOMINEES

BEST PICTURE
PRODUCTION
(Most popular picture)

★ **WINGS**
7TH HEAVEN
THE RACKET

BEST PICTURE
UNIQUE AND ARTISTIC PRODUCTION
(Most critically acclaimed picture)

★ **SUNRISE**
CHANG: A DRAMA OF THE WILDERNESS
THE CROWD

BEST ACTOR

★ **EMIL JANNINGS—The Last Command** *and*
The Way of All Flesh
RICHARD BARTHELMESS—The Noose *and*
The Patent Leather Kid

BEST ACTRESS

★ **JANET GAYNOR—7th Heaven** *and* **Street**
Angel *and* **Sunrise**
LOUISE DRESSER—A Ship Comes In
GLORIA SWANSON—Sadie Thompson

BEST DIRECTOR (DRAMA)

★ **7TH HEAVEN—Frank Borzage**
THE CROWD—King Vidor
SORRELL AND SON—Herbert Brenon

BEST DIRECTOR (COMEDY)

★ **TWO ARABIAN KNIGHTS—Lewis Milestone**
SPEEDY—Ted Wilde

BEST CINEMATOGRAPHY

★ **SUNRISE**
THE DEVIL DANCER
THE MAGIC FLAME
SADIE THOMPSON

BEST ART DIRECTION

★ **THE DOVE** *and* **TEMPEST**
7TH HEAVEN
SUNRISE

BEST WRITING (ADAPTATION)

★ **7TH HEAVEN HEAVEN**
GLORIOUS BETSY
THE JAZZ SINGER

BEST WRITING (ORIGINAL)

★ **UNDERWORLD**
THE LAST COMMAND

BEST ENGINEERING EFFECTS

★ **WINGS**

SPECIAL AWARD

★ **THE CIRCUS (Charlie Chaplin actor, writer, director, producer)**
THE JAZZ SINGER (First sound movie)

1929

1930

Films released August 1928 thru July 1929.

BEST PICTURE

★ **THE BROADWAY MELODY**
ALIBI
THE HOLLYWOOD REVUE OF 1929
IN OLD ARIZONA
THE PATRIOT

ACTOR

★ **WARNER BAXTER—In Old Arizona**
GEORGE BANCROFT—Thunderbolt
CHESTER MORRIS—Alibi
PAUL MUNI—The Valiant
LEWIS STONE—The Patriot

ACTRESS

★ **MARY PICKFORD—Coquette**
RUTH CHATTERTON—Madame X
BETTY COMPSON—The Barker
JEANNE EAGELS—The Letter
CORINNE GRIFFITH—The Divine Lady
BESSIE LOVE—The Broadway Melody

DIRECTOR

★ **THE DIVINE LADY—Frank Lloyd**
THE BROADWAY MELODY—Harry Beaumont
DRAG—Frank Lloyd
IN OLD ARIZONA—Irving Cummings
MADAME X—Lionel Barrymore
THE PATRIOT—Ernst Lubitsch
WEARY RIVER—Frank Lloyd

CINEMATOGRAPHY

★ **WHITE SHADOWS IN THE SOUTH SEAS**
THE DIVINE LADY
FOUR DEVILS
IN OLD ARIZONA
OUR DANCING DAUGHTERS
STREET ANGEL

ART DIRECTION

★ **THE BRIDGE OF SAN LUIS REY**
ALIBI
THE AWAKENING
DYNAMITE
THE PATRIOT
STREET ANGEL

WRITING

★ **THE PATRIOT**
THE COP
IN OLD ARIZONA
THE LAST OF MRS. CHEYNEY
THE LEATHERNECK
OUR DANCING DAUGHTERS
SAL OF SINGAPORE
SKYSCRAPER
THE VALIANT
A WOMAN OF AFFAIRS
WONDER OF WOMEN

1931

Films released August 1929 thru July 1930.
(Ceremony held in November, 1930)

BEST PICTURE

★ **ALL QUIET ON THE WESTERN FRONT**
THE BIG HOUSE
DISRAELI
THE DIVORCEE
THE LOVE PARADE

ACTOR

★ **GEORGE ARLISS—Disraeli**
GEORGE ARLISS—The Green Goddess
WALLACE BEERY—The Big House
MAURICE CHEVALIER—The Big Pond
MAURICE CHEVALIER—The Love Parade
RONALD COLMAN—Bulldog Drummond
RONALD COLMAN—Condemned
LAWRENCE TIBBETT—The Rogue Song

ACTRESS

★ **NORMA SHEARER—The Divorcee**
NANCY CARROLL—The Devil's Holiday
RUTH CHATTERTON—Sarah and Son
GRETA GARBO—Anna Christie
GRETA GARBO—Romance
NORMA SHEARER—Their Own Desire
GLORIA SWANSON—The Trespasser

DIRECTOR

★ **ALL QUIET ON THE WESTERN FRONT—Lewis Milestone**
ANNA CHRISTIE—Clarence Brown
THE DIVORCEE—Robert Leonard
HALLELUJAH—King Vidor
THE LOVE PARADE—Ernst Lubitsch
ROMANCE—Clarence Brown

CINEMATOGRAPHY

★ **WITH BYRD AT THE SOUTH POLE**
ALL QUIET ON THE WESTERN FRONT
ANNA CHRISTIE
HELL'S ANGELS
THE LOVE PARADE

ART DIRECTION

★ **KING OF JAZZ**
BULLDOG DRUMMOND
THE LOVE PARADE
SALLY
THE VAGABOND KING

WRITING

★ **THE BIG HOUSE**
ALL QUIET ON THE WESTERN FRONT
DISRAELI
THE DIVORCEE
STREET OF CHANCE

SOUND RECORDING

★ **THE BIG HOUSE**
THE CASE OF SERGEANT GRISCHA
THE LOVE PARADE
RAFFLES
SONG OF THE FLAME

1932

Films released August 1930 thru July 1931.

BEST PICTURE

★ **CIMARRON**
EAST LYNNE
THE FRONT PAGE
SKIPPY
TRADER HORN

ACTOR

★ **LIONEL BARRYMORE—A Free Soul**
JACKIE COOPER—Skippy
RICHARD DIX—Cimarron
FREDRIC MARCH—The Royal Family of Broadway
ADOLPHE MENJOU—The Front Page

ACTRESS

★ **MARIE DRESSLER—Min and Bill**
MARLENE DIETRICH—Morocco
IRENE DUNNE—Cimarron
ANN HARDING—Holiday
NORMA SHEARER—A Free Soul

DIRECTOR

★ **SKIPPY—Norman Taurog**
A FREE SOUL—Clarence Brown
THE FRONT PAGE—Lewis Milestone
CIMARRON—Wesley Ruggles
MOROCCO—Joseph von Sternberg

CINEMATOGRAPHY

★ **TABU—Floyd Crosby**
CIMARRON—Edward Cronjager
MOROCCO—Lee Garmes
THE RIGHT TO LOVE—Charles Lang
SVENGALI—Barney McGill

ART DIRECTION

★ **CIMARRON**
JUST IMAGINE
MOROCCO
SVENGALI
WHOOPEE!

ORIGINAL STORY

★ **THE DAWN PATROL**
THE DOORWAY TO HELL
LAUGHTER
THE PUBLIC ENEMY
SMART MONEY

ADAPTED SCREENPLAY

★ **CIMARRON**
THE CRIMINAL CODE
HOLIDAY
LITTLE CAESAR
SKIPPY

SOUND RECORDING

★ **PARAMOUNT PUBLIX STUDIO SOUND
DEPARTMENT**
MGM STUDIO SOUND DEPARTMENT
RKO RADIO STUDIO SOUND DEPARTMENT
SAMUEL GOLDWYN-UNITED ARTIST STUDIO SOUND
DEPARTMENT

1933

Films released August 1931 thru July 1932.

BEST PICTURE

★ **GRAND HOTEL**
 ARROWSMITH
 BAD GIRL
 THE CHAMP
 FIVE STAR FINAL
 ONE HOUR WITH YOU
 SHANGHAI EXPRESS
 THE SMILING LIEUTENANT

ACTOR

★ **WALLACE BEERY—The Champ**
★ **FREDRIC MARCH—Dr. Jekyll and Mr. Hyde**
   (Tied)
 ALFRED LUNT—The Guardsman

ACTRESS

★ **HELEN HAYES—The Sin of Madelon Caudet**
 MARIE DRESSLER—Emma
 LYNN FONTANNE—The Guardsman

DIRECTOR

★ **BAD GIRL—Frank Borzage**
 THE CHAMP—King Vidor
 SHANGHAI EXPRESS—Josef von Sternberg

CINEMATOGRAPHY

★ **SHANGHAI EXPRESS—Lee Garmes**
ARROWSMITH—Ray June
DR. JEKYLL AND MR. HYDE—Karl Struss

ART DIRECTION

★ **TRANSATLANTIC**
À NOUS LA LIBERTÉ (Freedom for Us)
ARROWSMITH

ORIGINAL STORY

★ **THE CHAMP**
LADY AND GENT
THE STAR WITNESS
WHAT PRICE HOLLYWOOD?

ADAPTED SCREENPLAY

★ **BAD GIRL**
ARROWSMITH
DR. JEKYLL AND MR. HYDE

SOUND RECORDING

★ **PARAMOUNT PUBLIX STUDIO SOUND DEPARTMENT**
MGM STUDIO SOUND DEPARTMENT
RKO RADIO STUDIO SOUND DEPARTMENT
WALT DISNEY PRODUCTIONS
WARNER BROS. FIRST NATIONAL STUDIO SOUND DEPARTMENT

1934

Films released August 1932 thru December 1933;
Hays Code begins film censorship enforcment.

BEST PICTURE

★ **CAVALCADE**
42nd STREET
A FAREWELL TO ARMS
I AM A FUGITIVE FROM A CHAIN GANG
LADY FOR A DAY
LITTLE WOMEN
THE PRIVATE LIFE OF HENRY VIII
SHE DONE HIM WRONG
SMILIN' THROUGH
STATE FAIR

ACTOR

★ **CHARLES LAUGHTON—The Private Life of Henry VIII**
LESLIE HOWARD—Berkeley Square
PAUL MUNI—I Am a Fugitive from a Chain Gang

ACTRESS

★ **KATHARINE HEPBURN—Morning Glory**
MAY ROBSON—Lady for a Day
DIANA WYNYARD—Cavalcade

DIRECTOR

★ **CAVALCADE—Frank Lloyd**
LADY FOR A DAY—Frank Capra
LITTLE WOMEN—George Cukor

CINEMATOGRAPHY

★ **A FAREWELL TO ARMS—Charles Lang**
REUNION IN VIENNA—George J. Folsey
SIGN OF THE CROSS—Karl Struss

ART DIRECTION

★ **CAVALCADE**
A FAREWELL TO ARMS
WHEN LADIES MEET

ORIGINAL STORY

★ **ONE WAY PASSAGE**
THE PRIZEFIGHTER AND THE LADY
RASPUTIN AND THE EMPRESS

ADAPTED SCREENPLAY

★ **LITTLE WOMEN**
LADY FOR A DAY
STATE FAIR

SOUND RECORDING

★ **A FAREWELL TO ARMS**
42nd STREET
GOLD DIGGERS OF 1933
I AM A FUGITIVE FROM A CHAIN GANG

1935

Henceforth, Academy Awards honor previous year's releases.

*Davis wins so many write-in votes that the Academy, which originally denies her nomination, is forced to change its mind.

BEST PICTURE

★ **IT HAPPENED ONE NIGHT**
  THE BARRETTS OF WIMPOLE STREET
  CLEOPATRA
  FLIRTATION WALK
  THE GAY DIVORCEE
  HERE COMES THE NAVY
  THE HOUSE OF ROTHSCHILD
  IMITATION OF LIFE
  ONE NIGHT OF LOVE
  THE THIN MAN
  VIVA VILLA!
  THE WHITE PARADE

ACTOR

★ **CLARK GABLE—It Happened One Night**
  FRANK MORGAN—The Affairs of Cellini
  WILLIAM POWELL—The Thin Man

ACTRESS

★ **CLAUDETTE COLBERT—It Happened One Night**
  BETTE DAVIS—Of Human Bondage*
  GRACE MOORE—One Night of Love
  NORMA SHEARER—The Barretts of Wimpole Street

DIRECTOR

★ **IT HAPPENED ONE NIGHT—Frank Capra**
  ONE NIGHT OF LOVE—Victor Schertzinger
  THE THIN MAN—W.S. Van Dyke

CINEMATOGRAPHY

★ **CLEOPATRA—Victor Milner**
THE AFFAIRS OF CELLINI—Charles Rosher
OPERATOR 13—George J. Folsey

FILM EDITING

★ **ESKIMO**
CLEOPATRA
ONE NIGHT OF LOVE

ART DIRECTION

★ **THE MERRY WIDOW**
THE AFFAIRS OF CELLINI
THE GAY DIVORCEE

ORIGINAL STORY

★ **MANHATTAN MELODRAMA**
HIDE-OUT
THE RICHEST GIRL IN THE WORLD

ADAPTED SCREENPLAY

★ **IT HAPPENED ONE NIGHT**
THE THIN MAN
VIVA VILLA!

SCORE

★ **ONE NIGHT OF LOVE**
THE GAY DIVORCEE
THE LOST PATROL

SONG

★ **THE CONTINENTAL** *from* **The Gay Divorcee**
CARIOCA *from* Flying Down to Rio
LOVE IN BLOOM *from* She Loves Me Not

1936

BEST PICTURE

★ **MUTINY ON THE BOUNTY**
ALICE ADAMS
BROADWAY MELODY OF 1936
CAPTAIN BLOOD
DAVID COPPERFIELD
THE INFORMER
LES MISÉRABLES
THE LIVES OF A BENGAL LANCER
A MIDSUMMER NIGHT'S DREAM
NAUGHTY MARIETTA
RUGGLES OF RED GAP
TOP HAT

ACTOR

★ **VICTOR McLAGLEN—The Informer**
CLARK GABLE—Mutiny on the Bounty
CHARLES LAUGHTON—Mutiny on the Bounty
PAUL MUNI—Black Fury
FRANCHOT TONE—Mutiny on the Bounty

ACTRESS

★ **BETTE DAVIS—Dangerous**
ELISABETH BERGNER—Escape Me Never
KATHARINE HEPBURN—Alice Adams
MIRIAM HOPKINS—Becky Sharp
MERLE OBERON—The Dark Angel

DIRECTOR

★ **THE INFORMER—John Ford**
CAPTAIN BLOOD—Michael Curtiz
THE LIVES OF A BENGAL LANCER—Henry Hathaway
MUTINY ON THE BOUNTY—Frank Lloyd

CINEMATOGRAPHY

★ **A MIDSUMMER NIGHT'S DREAM—Hal Mohr***
BARBARY COAST—Ray June
THE CRUSADES—Victor Milner
LES MISÉRABLES—Gregg Toland

FILM EDITING

★ **A MIDSUMMER NIGHT'S DREAM**
DAVID COPPERFIELD
THE INFORMER
THE LIVES OF A BENGAL LANCER
LES MISÉRABLES
MUTINY ON THE BOUNTY

ART DIRECTION

★ **THE DARK ANGEL**
THE LIVES OF A BENGAL LANCER
TOP HAT

ORIGINAL STORY

★ **THE SCOUNDREL**
BROADWAY MELODY OF 1936
G MEN
THE GAY DECEPTION

ADAPTED SCREENPLAY

★ **THE INFORMER**
CAPTAIN BLOOD
THE LIVES OF A BENGAL LANCER
MUTINY ON THE BOUNTY

SCORE

★ **THE INFORMER**
CAPTAIN BLOOD
MUTINY ON THE BOUNTY
PETER IBBETSON

SONG

★ **LULLABY OF BROADWAY** *from* **Gold Diggers of 1935**
CHEEK TO CHEEK *from* Top Hat
LOVELY TO LOOK AT *from* Roberta

1937

Supporting Actors categories added this year.

BEST PICTURE

★ **THE GREAT ZIEGFELD**
ANTHONY ADVERSE
DODSWORTH
LIBELED LADY
MR. DEEDS GOES TO TOWN
ROMEO AND JULIET
SAN FRANCISCO
THE STORY OF LOUIS PASTEUR
A TALE OF TWO CITIES
THREE SMART GIRLS

ACTOR

★ **PAUL MUNI—The Story of Louis Pasteur**
GARY COOPER—Mr. Deeds Goes to Town
WALTER HUSTON—Dodsworth
WILLIAM POWELL—My Man Godfrey
SPENCER TRACY—San Francisco

ACTRESS

★ **LUISE RAINER—The Great Ziegfeld**
IRENE DUNNE—Theodora Goes Wild
GLADYS GEORGE—Valiant is the Word for Carrie
CAROLE LOMBARD—My Man Godfrey
NORMA SHEARER—Romeo and Juliet

SUPPORTING ACTOR

★ **WALTER BRENNAN—Come and Get It**
MISCHA AUER—My Man Godfrey
STUART ERWIN—Pigskin Parade
BASIL RATHBONE—Romeo and Juliet
AKIM TAMIROFF—The General Died at Dawn

SUPPORTING ACTRESS

★ **GALE SONDERGAARD—Anthony Adverse**
BEULAH BONDI—The Gorgeous Hussy
ALICE BRADY—My Man Godfrey
BONITA GRANVILLE—These Three
MARIA OUSPENSKAYA—Dodsworth

DIRECTOR

★ **MR. DEEDS GOES TO TOWN—Frank Capra**
DODSWORTH—William Wyler
THE GREAT ZIEGFELD—Robert Z. Leonard MY MAN
GODFREY—Gregory La Cava
SAN FRANCISCO—W.S. Van Dyke

CINEMATOGRAPHY

★ **ANTHONY ADVERSE—Tony Gaudio**
THE GENERAL DIED AT DAWN—Victor Milner
THE GORGEOUS HUSSY—George Folsey

FILM EDITING

★ **ANTHONY ADVERSE**
COME AND GET IT
THE GREAT ZIEGFIELD
LLOYD'S OF LONDON
A TALE OF TWO CITIES
THEODORA GOES WILD

ART DIRECTION

★ **DODSWORTH**
ANTHONY ADVERSE
THE GREAT ZIEGFELD
LLOYD'S OF LONDON
THE MAGNIFICENT BRUTE
ROMEO AND JULIET
WINTERSET

SCORE

★ **ANTHONY ADVERSE**
THE CHARGE OF THE LIGHT BRIGADE
THE GARDEN OF ALLAH
THE GENERAL DIED AT DAWN
WINTERSET

SONG

★ **THE WAY YOU LOOK TONIGHT** *from* **Swing Time**
DID I REMEMBER *from* Suzy
I'VE GOT YOU UNDER MY SKIN *from* Born to Dance
A MELODY FROM THE SKY *from* Trail of the Lonesome Pine
PENNIES FROM HEAVEN *from* Pennies from Heaven
WHEN DID YOU LEAVE HEAVEN *from* Sing, Baby Sing

1938

Honorary award goes to world's first animated feature film, Disney's
SNOW WHITE AND THE SEVEN DWARFS *(one statuette & 7 miniatures).*

BEST PICTURE

★ **THE LIFE OF EMILE ZOLA**
THE AWFUL TRUTH
CAPTAINS COURAGEOUS
DEAD END
THE GOOD EARTH
IN OLD CHICAGO
LOST HORIZON
ONE HUNDRED MEN AND A GIRL
STAGE DOOR
A STAR IS BORN

ACTOR

★ **SPENCER TRACY—Captains Courageous**
CHARLES BOYER—Conquest
FREDRIC MARCH—A Star is Born
ROBERT MONTGOMERY—Night Must Fall
PAUL MUNI—The Life of Emile Zola

ACTRESS

★ **LUISE RAINER—The Good Earth**
IRENE DUNNE—The Awful Truth
GRETA GARBO—Camille
JANET GAYNOR—A Star is Born
BARBARA STANWYCK—Stella Dallas

SUPPORTING ACTOR

★ **JOSEPH SCHILDKRAUT—The Life of Emile Zola**
RALPH BELLAMY—The Awful Truth
THOMAS MITCHELL—The Hurricane
H.B. WARNER—Lost Horizon
ROLAND YOUNG—Topper

SUPPORTING ACTRESS

★ **ALICE BRADY—In Old Chicago**
ANDREA LEEDS—Stage Door
ANNE SHIRLEY—Stella Dallas
CLAIRE TREVOR—Dead End
DAME MAY WHITTY—Night Must Fall

DIRECTOR

★ **THE AWFUL TRUTH—Leo McCarey**
THE GOOD EARTH—Sidney Franklin
THE LIFE OF EMILE ZOLA—William Dieterle
STAGE DOOR—Gregory La Cava
A STAR IS BORN—William Wellman

CINEMATOGRAPHY

★ **THE GOOD EARTH—Karl Freund**
DEAD END—Gregg Toland
WINGS OVER HONOLULU—Joseph Valentine

FILM EDITING

★ **LOST HORIZON**
THE AWFUL TRUTH
CAPTAINS COURAGEOUS
THE GOOD EARTH
ONE HUNDRED MEN AND A GIRL

SCORE

★ **ONE HUNDRED MEN AND A GIRL**
THE HURRUCANE
IN OLD CHICAGO
THE LIFE OF EMILE ZOLA
LOST HORIZON
MAKE A WISH
MAYTIME
PORTIA ON TRIAL
THE PRISONER OF ZENDA
QUALITY STREET
SNOW WHITE AND THE SEVEN DWARFS
SOMETHING TO SING ABOUT
SOULS AT SEA
WAY OUT WEST

SONG

★ **SWEET LEILANI** *from* **Waikiki Wedding**
REMEMBER ME *from* Mr. Dodd Takes the Air
THAT OLD FEELING *from* Walter Wanger's Vogues
of 1938
THEY CAN'T TAKE THAT AWAY FROM ME *from* Shall
We Dance
WHISPERS IN THE DARK *from* Artists and Models

1939

The "Academy Award of Merit" adopts OSCAR title.

BEST PICTURE

★ **YOU CAN'T TAKE IT WITH YOU**
   THE ADVENTURES OF ROBIN HOOD
   ALEXANDER'S RAGTIME BAND
   BOYS TOWN
   THE CITADEL
   FOUR DAUGHTERS
   LA GRANDE ILLUSION
   JEZEBEL
   PYGMALION
   TEST PILOT

ACTOR

★ **SPENCER TRACY—Boys Town**
   CHARLES BOYER—Algiers
   JAMES CAGNEY—Angels With Dirty Faces
   ROBERT DONAT—The Citadel
   LESLIE HOWARD—Pygmalion

ACTRESS

★ **BETTE DAVIS—Jezebel**
   FAY BAINTER—White Banners
   WENDY HILLER—Pygmalion
   NORMA SHEARER—Marie Antoinette
   MARGARET SULLAVAN—Three Comrades

SUPPORTING ACTOR

★ **WALTER BRENNAN—Kentucky**
   JOHN GARFIELD—Four Daughters
   GENE LOCKHART—Algiers
   ROBERT MORLEY—Marie Antoinette
   BASIL RATHBONE—If I Were King

SUPPORTING ACTRESS

★ **FAY BAINTER—Jezebel**
   BEULAH BONDI—Of Human Hearts
   BILLIE BURKE—Merrily We Live
   SPRING BYINGTON—You Can't Take It With You
   MILIZA KORJUS—The Great Waltz

DIRECTOR

★ **YOU CAN'T TAKE IT WITH YOU—Frank Capra**
ANGELS WITH DIRTY FACES—Michael Curtiz
BOYS TOWN—Norman Taurog
THE CITADEL—King Vidor
FOUR DAUGHTERS—Michael Curtiz

CINEMATOGRAPHY

★ **THE GREAT WALTZ—Joseph Ruttenberg**
ALGIERS—James Wong Howe
ARMY GIRL—Ernest Miller and Harry Wild
THE BUCCANEER—Victor Milner
JEZEBEL—Ernest Haller
MAD ABOUT MUSIC—Joseph Valentine
MERRILY WE LIVE—Norbert Brodine SUEZ—Peverell Marley
VIVACIOUS LADY—Robert de Grasse
YOU CAN'T TAKE IT WITH YOU—Joseph Walker
THE YOUNG IN HEART—Leon Shamroy

ORIGINAL SCORE

★ **THE ADVENTURES OF ROBIN HOOD—Erich W. Korngold**
ARMY GIRL—Victor Young
BLOCKADE—Werner Janssen
BLOCK-HEADS—Marvin Hatley
BREAKING THE ICE—Victor Young
THE COWBOY AND THE LADY—Alfred Newman
IF I WERE KING—Richard Hageman
MARIE ANTOINETTE—Herbert Stothart
PACIFIC LINER—Russell Bennett
SUEZ—Louis Silvers
THE YOUNG IN HEART—Franz Waxman

SONG

★ **THANKS FOR THE MEMORY** *from* **The Big Broadcast of 1938**
ALWAYS AND ALWAYS *from* Mannequin
CHANGE PARTNERS *from* Carefree
THE COWBOY AND THE LADY *from* The Cowboy and the Lady
DUST *from* Under Western Stars
JEEPERS CREEPERS *from* Going Places
MERRILY WE LIVE *from* Merrily We Live
A MIST OVER THE MOON *from* The Lady Objects
MY OWN *from* That Certain Age
NOW IT CAN BE TOLD *from* Alexander's Ragtime Band

1940

McDaniel First African American to win Oscar.

First filmed event brings out glamorous gowns, furs, and jewelry.

BEST PICTURE

★ **GONE WITH THE WIND**
  DARK VICTORY
  GOODBYE, MR. CHIPS
  LOVE AFFAIR
  MR. SMITH GOES TO WASHINGTON
  NINOTCHKA
  OF MICE AND MEN
  STAGECOACH
  THE WIZARD OF OZ
  WUTHERING HEIGHTS

ACTOR

★ **ROBERT DONAT—Goodbye, Mr. Chips**
  CLARK GABLE—Gone with the Wind
  LAURENCE OLIVIER—Wuthering Heights
  MICKEY ROONEY—Babes in Arms
  JAMES STEWART—Mr. Smith Goes to Washington

ACTRESS

★ **VIVIEN LEIGH—Gone with the Wind**
  BETTE DAVIS—Dark Victory
  IRENE DUNNE—Love Affair
  GRETA GARBO—Ninotchka
  GREER GARSON—Goodbye, Mr. Chips

SUPPORTING ACTOR

★ **THOMAS MITCHELL—Stagecoach**
  BRIAN AHERNE—Juarez
  HARRY CAREY—Mr. Smith Goes to Washington
  BRIAN DONLEVY—Beau Geste
  CLAUDE RAINS—Mr. Smith Goes to Washington

SUPPORTING ACTRESS

★ **HATTIE McDANIEL—Gone with the Wind***
  OLIVIA de HAVILLAND—Gone with the Wind
  GERALDINE FITZGERALD—Wuthering Heights
  EDNA MAY OLIVER—Drums Along the Mohawk
  MARIA OUSPENSKAYA—Love Affair

DIRECTOR

★ **GONE WITH THE WIND—Victor Fleming**
GOODBYE, MR. CHIPS—Sam Wood
MR. SMITH GOES TO WASHINGTON—Frank Capra
STAGECOACH—John Ford
WUTHERING HEIGHTS—William Wyler

CINEMATOGRAPHY (BLACK & WHITE)

★ **WUTHERING HEIGHTS—Gregg Toland**
FIRST LOVE—Joseph Valentine
THE GREAT VICTOR HERBERT—Victor Milner
GUNGA DIN—Joseph H. August
INTERMEZZO—Gregg Toland
JUAREZ—Tony Gaudio
LADY OF THE TROPICS—Norbert Broding
OF MICE AND MEN—George Folsey
ONLY ANGELS HAVE WINGS—Joseph Walker
THE RAINS CAME—Arthur Charles Miller
STAGECOACH—Bert Glennon

ORIGINAL SCORE

★ **THE WIZARD OF OZ—Herbert Stothart**
DARK VICTORY—Max Steiner
ETERNALLY YOURS—Werner Janssen
GOLDEN BOY—Victor Young
GONE WITH THE WIND—Max Steiner
GULLIVER'S TRAVELS—Victor Young
THE MAN IN THE IRON MASK—Lud Gluskin and Lucien
Moraweck
MAN OF CONQUEST—Victor Young
NURSE EDITH CAVELL—Anthony Collins
OF MICE AND MEN—Aaron Copland
THE RAINS CAME—Alfred Newman
WUTHERING HEIGHTS—Alfred Newman

SONG

★ **OVER THE RAINBOW** *from* **The Wizard of Oz**
FAITHFUL FOREVER *from* Gulliver's Travels
I POURED MY HEART INTO A SONG *from* Second Fiddle
WISHING *from* Love Affair

Cocoanut Grove, Los Angeles   February 29, 1940

1941

First time sealed envelopes deliver winning names.

BEST PICTURE

★ **REBECCA**
ALL THIS, AND HEAVEN TOO
FOREIGN CORRESPONDENT
THE GRAPES OF WRATH
THE GREAT DICTATOR
KITTY FOYLE
THE LETTER
THE LONG VOYAGE HOME
OUR TOWN
THE PHILADELPHIA STORY

ACTOR

★ **JAMES STEWART—The Philadelphia Story**
CHARLES CHAPLIN—The Great Dictator
HENRY FONDA—The Grapes of Wrath
RAYMOND MASSEY—Abe Lincoln in Illinois
LAURENCE OLIVIER—Rebecca

ACTRESS

★ **GINGER ROGERS—Kitty Foyle**
BETTE DAVIS—The Letter
JOAN FONTAINE—Rebecca
KATHARINE HEPBURN—The Philadelphia Story
MARTHA SCOTT—Our Town

SUPPORTING ACTOR

★ **WALTER BRENNAN—The Westerner**
ALBERT BASSERMANN—Foreign Correspondent
WILLIAM GARGAN—They Knew What They Wanted
JACK OAKIE—The Great Dictator
JAMES STEPHENSON—The Letter

SUPPORTING ACTRESS

★ **JANE DARWELL—The Grapes of Wrath**
JUDITH ANDERSON—Rebecca
RUTH HUSSEY—The Philadelphia Story
BARBARA O'NEIL—All This, and Heaven Too
MARJORIE RAMBEAU—Primrose Path

DIRECTOR

★ **THE GRAPES OF WRATH—John Ford**
   KITTY FOYLE—Sam Wood
   THE LETTER—William Wyler
   THE PHILADELPHIA STORY—George Cukor
   REBECCA—Alfred Hitchcock

CINEMATOGRAPHY (BLACK & WHITE)

★ **REBECCA—George Barnes**
   ABE LINCOLN IN ILLINOIS—James Wong Howe
   ALL THIS, AND HEAVEN TOO—Ernest Haller
   ARISE, MY LOVE—Charles Lang
   BOOM TOWN—Harold Rossen
   FOREIGN CORRESPONDENT—Rudolph Maté
   THE LETTER—Gaetano Gaudio
   THE LONG VOYAGE HOME—Gregg Toland
   SPRING PARADE—Joseph Valentine
   WATERLOO BRIDGE—Joseph Ruttenberg

ORIGINAL SCORE

★ **PINOCCHIO—Leigh Harline, Paul J. Smith, Ned Washington**
   ARIZONA—Victor Young
   DARK COMMAND—Victor Young
   THE FIGHT FOR LIFE—Louis Gruenberg
   THE GREAT DICTATOR—Meredith Willson
   THE HOUSE OF THE SEVEN GABLES—Frank Skinner
   THE HOWARDS OF VIRGINIA—Richard Hageman
   THE LETTER—Max Steiner
   THE LONG VOYAGE HOME—Richard Hageman
   THE MARK OF ZORRO—Alfred Newman
   MY FAVORITE WIFE—Roy Webb
   NORTH WEST MOUNTED POLICE—Victor Young
   ONE MILLION B.C.—Werner Heymann
   OUR TOWN—Aaron Copland
   REBECCA—Franz Waxman
   THE THIEF OF BAGDAD—Miklós Rózsa
   WATERLOO BRIDGE—Herbert Stothart

SONG

★ **WHEN YOU WISH UPON A STAR** *from* **Pinocchio**
   DOWN ARGENTINE WAY *from* Down Argentine Way
   I'D KNOW YOU ANYWHERE *from* You'll Find Out
   IT'S A BLUE WORLD *from* Music in My Heart
   LOVE OF MY LIFE *from* Second Chorus
   ONLY FOREVER *from* Rhythm on the River
   OUR LOVE AFFAIR *from* Strike Up the Band
   WALTZING IN THE CLOUDS *from* Spring Parade
   WHO AM I? *from* Hit Parade of 1941

1942

Documentary category added.

BEST PICTURE

★ **HOW GREEN WAS MY VALLEY**
  BLOSSOMS IN THE DUST
  CITIZEN KANE
  HERE COMES MR. JORDAN
  HOLD BACK THE DAWN
  THE LITTLE FOXES
  THE MALTESE FALCON
  ONE FOOT IN HEAVEN
  SERGEANT YORK
  SUSPICION

ACTOR

★ **GARY COOPER—Sergeant York**
  CARY GRANT—Penny Serenade
  WALTER HUSTON—All That Money Can Buy
  ROBERT MONTGOMERY—Here Comes Mr. Jordan
  ORSON WELLS—Citizen Kane

ACTRESS

★ **JOAN FONTAINE—Suspicion**
  BETTE DAVIS—The Little Foxes
  OLIVIA de HAVILLAND—Hold Back the Dawn
  GREER GARSON—Blossoms in the Dust
  BARBARA STANWICK—Ball of Fire

SUPPORTING ACTOR

★ **DONALD CRISP—How Green Was My Valley**
  WALTER BRENNAN—Sergeant York
  CHARLES COBURN—The Devil and Miss Jones
  JAMES GLEASON—Here Comes Mr. Jordan
  SYDNEY GREENSTREET—The Maltese Falcon

SUPPORTING ACTRESS

★ **MARY ASTOR—The Great Lie**
  SARA ALLGOOD—How Green Was My Valley
  PATRICIA COLLINGE—The Little Foxes
  TERESA WRIGHT—The Little Foxes
  MARGARET WYCHERLY—Sergeant York

DIRECTOR

★ **HOW GREEN WAS MY VALLEY—John Ford**
CITIZEN KANE—Orson Welles
HERE COMES MR. JORDAN—Alexander Hall
THE LITTLE FOXES—William Wyler
SERGEANT YORK—Howard Hawks

CINEMATOGRAPHY (BLACK & WHITE)

★ **HOW GREEN WAS MY VALLEY—Arthur C. Miller**
CITIZEN KANE—Gregg Toland
THE CHOCOLATE SOLDIER—Karl Freund
DR. JEKYLL AND MR. HYDE—Joseph Ruttenberg
HERE COMES MR. JORDAN—Joseph Walker
HOLD BACK THE DAWN—Leo Tover
SERGEANT YORK—Sol Polito
SUN VALLEY SERENADE—Edward Cronjager
SUNDOWN—Charles Lang
THAT HAMILTON WOMAN—Rudolph Maté

DRAMATIC SCORE

★ **ALL THAT MONEY CAN BUY—Bernard Herrmann**
BACK STREET—Frank Skinner
BALL OF FIRE—Alfred Newman
CITIZEN KANE—Bernard Herrmann
DR. JEKYLL AND MR. HYDE—Franz Waxman
HOLD BACK THE DAWN—Victor Young
HOW GREEN WAS MY VALLEY—Alfred Newman
THE LITTLE FOXES—Meredith Willson
SERGEANT YORK—Max Steiner
SUSPICION—Franz Waxman
~ 10 additional nominees

MUSICAL SCORE

★ **DUMBO—Frank Churchill and Oliver Wallace**
BIRTH OF THE BLUES—Robert Emmett Dolan
BUCK PRIVATES—Charles Previn
THE CHOCOLATE SOLDIER—Herbert Stothart & Bronislau Kaper
THE STRAWBERRY BLONDE—Heinz Roemheld
SUN VALLEY SERENADE—Emil Newman
~ 4 additional nominees

SONG

★ **THE LAST TIME I SAW PARIS** *from* **Lady Be Good**
BABY MINE *from* Dumbo
BLUES IN THE NIGHT *from* Blues in the Night
BOOGIE WOOGIE BUGLE BOY OF COMPANY B *from*
  Buck Privates
CHATTANOOGA CHOO CHOO *from* Sun Valley Serenade
~ 4 additional nominees

1943

Garson's rambling 6-minute acceptance inspires 45-second rule.

BEST PICTURE

★ **MRS. MINIVER**
   49th PARALLEL
   KINGS ROW
   THE MAGNIFICENT AMBERSONS
   THE PIED PIPER
   THE PRIDE OF THE YANKEES
   RANDOM HARVEST
   THE TALK OF THE TOWN
   WAKE ISLAND
   YANKEE DOODLE DANDY

ACTOR

★ **JAMES CAGNEY—Yankee Doodle Dandy**
   RONALD COLMAN—Random Harvest
   GARY COOPER—The Pride of the Yankees
   WALTER PIDGEON—Mrs. Miniver
   MONTY WOOLLEY—The Pied Piper

ACTRESS

★ **GREER GARSON—Mrs. Miniver***
   BETTE DAVIS—Now, Voyager
   KATHARINE HEPBURN—Woman of the Year
   ROSALIND RUSSELL—My Sister Eileen
   TERESA WRIGHT—The Pride of the Yankees

SUPPORTING ACTOR

★ **VAN HEFLIN—Johnny Eager**
   WILLIAM BENDIX—Wake Island
   WALTER HUSTON—Yankee Doodle Dandy
   FRANK MORGAN—Tortilla Flat
   HENRY TRAVERS—Mrs. Miniver

SUPPORTING ACTRESS

★ **TERESA WRIGHT—Mrs. Miniver**
   GLADYS COOPER—Now, Voyager
   AGNES MOOREHEAD—The Magnificent Ambersons
   SUSAN PETERS—Random Harvest
   DAME MAY WHITTY—Mrs. Miniver

DIRECTOR

★ **MRS. MINIVER—William Wyler**
KINGS ROW—Sam Wood
RANDOM HARVEST—Mervyn LeRoy
WAKE ISLAND—John Farrow
YANKEE DOODLE DANDY—Michael Curtiz

CINEMATOGRAPHY (BLACK & WHITE)

★ **MRS. MINIVER—Joseph Ruttenberg**
KINGS ROW—James Wong How
THE MAGNIFICENT AMBERSONS—Stanley Cortez
MOONTIDE—Charles G. Clarke
THE PIED PIPER—Edward Cronjager
THE PRIDE OF THE YANKEES—Rudolph Maté
TAKE A LETTER, DARLING—John Mescall
THE TALK OF THE TOWN—Ted Tetzlaff
TEN GENTLEMEN FROM WEST POINT—Leon Shamroy
THIS ABOVE ALL—Arthur C. Miller

DRAMATIC SCORE

★ **NOW, VOYAGER—Max Steiner**
BAMBI—Frank Churchill and Edward Plumb
THE CORSICAN BROTHERS—Dimitri Tiomkin
I MARRIED A WITCH—Roy Webb
JUNGLE BOOK—Miklós Rózsa
THE PRIDE OF THE YANKEES—Leigh Harline
RANDOM HARVEST—Herbert Stothart
TO BE OR NOT TO BE—Werner Heymann
~ 10 additional nominees

MUSICAL SCORE

★ **YANKEE DOODLE DANDY—Ray Heindorf and Heinz Roemheld**
FLYING WITH MUSIC—Edward Ward
FOR ME AND MY GAL—Roger Edens and Georgie Stoll
HOLIDAY INN—Robert Emmett Dolan
IT STARTED WITH EVE—Charles Previn and Hans Salter
JOHNNY DOUGHBOY—Walter Scharf
MY GAL SAL—Alfred Newman
YOU WERE NEVER LOVELIER—Leigh Harline

SONG

★ **WHITE CHRISTMAS** *from* **Holiday Inn**
HOW ABOUT YOU? *from* Babes on Broadway
I'VE GOT A GAL IN KALAMAZOO *from* Orchestra Wives
I'VE HEARD THAT SONG BEFORE *from* Youth on Parade
LOVE IS A SONG *from* Bambi
~ 5 additional nominees

1944

*First large scale event; free passes to persons in uniform;
full size statuettes replace plaques for supporting wins.*

BEST PICTURE

★ **CASABLANCA**
  FOR WHOM THE BELL TOLLS
  HEAVEN CAN WAIT
  THE HUMAN COMEDY
  IN WHICH WE SERVE
  MADAME CURIE
  THE MORE THE MERRIER
  THE OX-BOW INCIDENT
  THE SONG OF BERNADETTE
  WATCH ON THE RHINE

ACTOR

★ **PAUL LUKAS—Watch on the Rhine**
  HUMPHREY BOGART—Casablanca
  GARY COOPER—For Whom the Bell Tolls
  WALTER PIDGEON—Madame Curie
  MICKEY ROONEY—The Human Comedy

ACTRESS

★ **JENNIFER JONES—The Song of Bernadette**
  JEAN ARTHUR—The More the Merrier
  INGRID BERGMAN—For Whom the Bell Tolls
  JOAN FONTAINE—The Constant Nymph
  GREER GARSON—Madame Curie

SUPPORTING ACTOR

★ **CHARLES COBURN—The More the Merrier**
  CHARLES BICKFORD—The Song of Bernadette
  J. CARROL NAISH—Sahara
  CLAUDE RAINS—Casablanca
  AKIM TAMIROFF—For Whom the Bell Tolls

SUPPORTING ACTRESS

★ **KATINA PAXINOU—For Whom the Bell Tolls**
  GLADYS COOPER—The Song of Bernadette
  PAULETTE GODDARD—So Proudly We Hail!
  ANNE REVERE—The Song of Bernadette
  LUCILE WATSON—Watch on the Rhine

DIRECTOR

★ **CASABLANCA—Michael Curtiz**
HEAVEN CAN WAIT—Ernst Lubitsch
THE HUMAN COMEDY—Clarence Brown
THE MORE THE MERRIER—George Stevens
THE SONG OF BERNADETTE—Henry King

CINEMATOGRAPHY (BLACK & WHITE)

★ **THE SONG OF BERNADETTE—Arthur C. Miller**
AIR FORCE—James Wong Howe, Elmer Dyer, Charles A. Marshall
CASABLANCA—Arthur Edeson
CORVETT K-225—Tony Gaudio
FIVE GRAVES TO CAIRO—John Seitz
THE HUMAN COMEDY—Harry Stradling
MADAME CURIE—Joseph Ruttenberg
THE NORTH STAR—James Wong Howe
SAHARA—Rudolph Maté
SO PROUDLY WE HAIL—Charles Lang

DRAMATIC SCORE

★ **THE SONG OF BERNADETTE—Alfred Newman**
CASABLANCA—Max Steiner THE NORTH STAR—Aaron Copland
FOR WHOM THE BELL TOLLS—Victor Young
LADY OF BURLESQUE—Arthur Lange
MADAME CURIE—Herbert Stothart
THE MOON AND SIXPENCE—Dimitri Tiomkin
~ 9 additional nominees

MUSICAL SCORE

★ **THIS IS THE ARMY—Ray Heindorf**
CONEY ISLAND—Alfred Newman
HIT PARADE OF 1943—Walter Scharf
PHANTOM OF THE OPERA—Edward Ward
SALUDOS AMIGOS—Edward H. Plumb, Paul J. Smith, Charles Wolcott
THE SKY'S THE LIMIT—Leigh Harline
STAGE DOOR CANTEEN—Frederic E. Rich
STAR SPANGLED RHYTHM—Robert Emmett Dolan
SOMETHING TO SHOUT ABOUT—Morris Stoloff
THOUSANDS CHEER—Herbert Stothart

SONG

★ **YOU'LL NEVER KNOW** *from* **Hello, Frisco, Hello**
THAT OLD BLACK MAGIC *from* Star Spangled Rhythm
HAPPINESS IS A THING CALLED JOE *from* Cabin in the Sky
MY SHINING HOUR *from* The Sky's the Limit
YOU'D BE SO NICE TO COME HOME TO *from* Something to Shout About
~ 5 additional nominees

1945

Rule change limits Best Picture nominees to five.

BEST PICTURE

★ **GOING MY WAY**
DOUBLE INDEMNITY
GASLIGHT
SINCE YOU WENT AWAY
WILSON

ACTOR

★ **BING CROSBY—Going My Way**
CHARLES BOYER—Gaslight
BARRY FITZGERALD—Going My Way
CARY GRANT—None but the Lonely Heart
ALEXANDER KNOX—Wilson

ACTRESS

★ **INGRID BERGMAN—Gaslight**
CLAUDETTE COLBERT—Since You Went Away
BETTE DAVIS—Mr. Skeffington
GREER GARSON—Mrs. Parkington
BARBARA STANWYCK—Double Indemnity

SUPPORTING ACTOR

★ **BARRY FITZGERALD—Going My Way**
HUME CRONYN—The Seventh Cross
CLAUDE RAINS—Mr. Skeffington
CLIFTON WEBB—Laura
MONTY WOOLLEY—Since You Went Away

SUPPORTING ACTRESS

★ **ETHEL BARRYMORE—None But the Lonely Heart**
JENNIFER JONES—Since You Went Away
ANGELA LANSBURY—Gaslight
ALINE MacMAHON—Dragon Seed
AGNES MOOREHEAD—Mrs. Parkington

DIRECTOR

★ **GOING MY WAY—Leo McCarey**
DOUBLE INDEMNITY—Billy Wilder
LAURA—Otto Preminger
LIFEBOAT—Alfred Hitchcock
WILSON—Henry King

CINEMATOGRAPHY (BLACK & WHITE)

★ **LAURA—Joseph LaShelle**
DOUBLE INDEMNITY—John F. Seitz
DRAGON SEED—Sidney Wagner
GASLIGHT—Joseph Ruttenberg
GOING MY WAY—Lionel Lindon
LIFEBOAT—Glen MacWilliams
SINCE YOU WENT AWAY—Stanley Cortez & Lee Garmes
THIRTY SECONDS OVER TOKYO—Robert Surtees &
     Harold Rossen
THE UNINVITED—Charles Lang
THE WHITE CLIFFS OF DOVER—George J. Folsey

DRAMATIC SCORE

★ **SINCE YOU WENT AWAY—Max Steiner**
THE ADVENTURES OF MARK TWAIN—Max Steiner
THE BRIDGE OF SAN LUIS REY—Dimitri Tiomkin
DOUBLE INDEMNITY--Miklós Rózsa
THE FIGHTING SEABEES—Walter Scharf and Roy Webb
THE HAIRY APE—Edward Paul and Michel Michelet
KISMET—Herbert Stothart
NONE BUT THE LONELY HEART—Hanns Eisler & C. Bakaleinikoff
     ~ 12 additional nominees

MUSICAL SCORE

★ **COVER GIRL—Morris Stoloff & Carmen Dragon**
BRAZIL—Walter Scharf
HOLLWOOD CANTEEN—Ray Heindorf
IRISH EYES ARE SMILING—Alfred Newman
KNICKERBOCKER HOLIDAY—Werner R. Heymann & Kurt Weill
LADY IN THE DARK—Robert Emmett Dolan
MEET ME IN ST. LOUIS—Georgie Stoll
     ~ 7 additional nominees

SONG

★ **SWINGING ON A STAR** *from* **Going My Way**
I COULDN'T SLEEP A WINK LAST NIGHT *from* Higher and Higher
I'LL WALK ALONE *from* Follow the Boys
LONG AGO AND FAR AWAY *from* Cover Girl
RIO DE JANEIRO *from* Brazil
THE TROLLEY SONG *from* Meet Me in St. Louis
     ~ 6 additional nominees

Grauman's Chinese Theater, Hollywood   March 15, 1945

1946

Post WWII gold-plated, bronze statuettes
replace wartime plaster ones.

BEST PICTURE

★ **THE LOST WEEKEND**
   ANCHORS AWEIGH
   THE BELLS OF ST. MARY'S
   MILDRED PIERCE
   SPELLBOUND

ACTOR

★ **RAY MILLAND—The Lost Weekend**
   BING CROSBY—The Bells of St. Mary's
   GENE KELLY—Anchors Aweigh
   GREGORY PECK—The Keys of the Kingdom
   CORNEL WILDE—A Song to Remember

ACTRESS

★ **JOAN CRAWFORD—Mildred Pierce**
   INGRID BERGMAN—The Bells of St. Mary's
   GREER GARSON—The Valley of Decision
   JENNIFER JONES—Love Letters
   GENE TIERNEY—Leave Her to Heaven

SUPPORTING ACTOR

★ **JAMES DUNN—A Tree Grows in Brooklyn**
   MICHAEL CHEKHOV—Spellbound
   JOHN DALL—The Corn Is Green
   ROBERT MITCHUM—The Story of G.I. Joe
   J. CARROL NAISH—A Medal for Benny

SUPPORTING ACTRESS

★ **ANNE REVERE—National Velvet**
   EVE ARDEN—Mildred Pierce
   ANN BLYTH—Mildred Pierce
   ANGELA LANSBURY—The Picture of Dorian Gray
   JOAN LORRING—The Corn Is Green

DIRECTOR

★ **THE LOST WEEKEND—Billy Wilder**
THE BELLS OF ST. MARY'S—Leo McCarey
NATIONAL VELVET—Clarence Brown
THE SOUTHERNER—Jean Renoir
SPELLBOUND—Alfred Hitchcock

CINEMATOGRAPHY (BLACK & WHITE)

★ **THE PICTURE OF DORIAN GRAY—Harry Stradling**
THE KEYS OF THE KINGDOM—Arthur C. Miller
THE LOST WEEKEND—John F. Seitz
MILDRED PIERCE—Ernest Haller
SPELLBOUND—George Barnes

DRAMATIC SCORE

★ **SPELLBOUND—Miklós Rózsa**
THE BELLS OF ST. MARY'S—Robert Emmett Dolan
CAPTAIN KIDD—Werner Janssen
THE KEYS OF THE KINGDOM—Alfred Newman
THE LOST WEEKEND—Miklós Rózsa
LOVE LETTERS—Victor Young
THE STORY OF G.I. Joe—Louis Applebaum & Ann Ronell
THE WOMAN IN THE WINDOW—Hugo Friedhofer and
 Arthur Lange
   ~ 13 additional nominees

MUSICAL SCORE

★ **ANCHORS AWEIGH—Georgie Stoll**
BELLE OF THE YUKON—Arthur Lang
INCENDIARY BLONDE—Robert Emmett Dolan
RHAPSODY IN BLUE—Ray Heindorf and Max Steiner
STATE FAIR—Charles Henderson and Alfred Newman
   ~ 7 additional nominees

SONG

★ **IT MIGHT AS WELL BE SPRING** *from* **State Fair**
ACCENTUATE THE POSITIVE *from* Here Come the Waves
I FALL IN LOVE TOO EASILY *from* Anchors Aweigh
LOVE LETTERS *from* Love Letters
SO IN LOVE *from* Wonder Man
   ~ 9 additional nominees

1947

Rule change limits nominees to five in all categories.

BEST PICTURE

★ **THE BEST YEARS OF OUR LIVES**
HENRY V
IT'S A WONDERFUL LIFE
THE RAZOR'S EDGE
THE YEARLING

ACTOR

★ **FREDRIC MARCH—The Best Years of Our Lives**
LAURENCE OLIVIER—Henry V
LARRY PARKS—The Jolson Story
GREGORY PECK—The Yearling
JAMES STEWART—It's a Wonderful Life

ACTRESS

★ **OLIVIA de HAVILLAND—To Each His Own**
CELIA JOHNSON—Brief Encounter
JENNIFER JONES—Duel in the Sun
ROSALIND RUSSELL—Sister Kenny
JANE WYMAN—The Yearling

SUPPORTING ACTOR

★ **HAROLD RUSSELL—The Best Years of Our Lives**
CHARLES COBURN—The Green Years
WILLIAM DEMAREST—The Jolson Story
CLAUDE RAINS—Notorious
CLIFTON WEBB—The Razor's Edge

SUPPORTING ACTRESS

★ **ANNE BAXTER—The Razor's Edge**
ETHEL BARRYMORE—The Spiral Staircase
LILLIAN GISH—Duel in the Sun
FLORA ROBSON—Saratoga Trunk
GALE SONDERGAARD—Anna and the King of Siam

DIRECTOR

★ **THE BEST YEARS OF OUR LIVES—William Wyler**
BRIEF ENCOUNTER—David Lean
IT'S A WONDERFUL LIFE—Frank Capra
THE KILLERS—Robert Siodmak
THE YEARLING—Clarence Brown

CINEMATOGRAPHY (BLACK & WHITE)

★ **ANNA AND THE KING OF SIAM—Arthur C. Miller**
THE GREEN YEARS—George Folsey

CINEMATOGRAPHY (COLOR)

★ **THE YEARLING—Charles Rosher, Leonard Smith, Arthur Arling**
THE JOLSON STORY—Joseph Walker

DRAMATIC SCORE

★ **THE BEST YEARS OF OUR LIVES—Hugo Friedhofer**
ANNA AND THE KING OF SIAM—Bernard Hermann
HENRY V—William Walton
HUMORESQUE—Franz Waxman
THE KILLERS—Miklós Rózsa

MUSICAL SCORE

★ **THE JOLSON STORY—Morris Stoloff**
BLUE SKIES—Robert Emmett Dolan
CENTENNIAL SUMMER—Alfred Newman
THE HARVEY GIRLS—Lennie Hayton
NIGHT AND DAY—Ray Heindorf and Max Steiner

SONG

★ **ON THE ATCHISON, TOPEKA, AND THE SANTA FE**
from **The Harvy Girls**
ALL THROUGH THE DAY *from* Centennial Summer
I CAN'T BEGIN TO TELL YOU *from* The Dolly Sisters
OLE BUTTERMILK SKY *from* Canyon Passage
YOU KEEP COMING BACK LIKE A SONG *from* Blue Skies

1948

Honorary (non-competitive) acting award goes to Black man, James Basket, for performance in Disney's SONG OF THE SOUTH (film now banned in U.S.).

BEST PICTURE

★ **GENTLEMAN'S AGREEMENT**
THE BISHOP'S WIFE
CROSSFIRE
GREAT EXPECTATIONS
MIRACLE ON 34th STREET

ACTOR

★ **RONALD COLMAN—A Double Life**
JOHN GARFIELD—Body and Soul
GREGORY PECK—Gentleman's Agreement
WILLIAM POWELL—Life with Father
MICHAEL REDGRAVE—Mourning Becomes Electra

ACTRESS

★ **LORETTA YOUNG—The Farmer's Daughter**
JOAN CRAWFORD—Possessed
SUSAN HAYWARD—Smash-Up, the Story of a Woman
DOROTHY McGUIRE—Gentleman's Agreement
ROSALIND RUSSELL—Mourning Becomes Electra

SUPPORTING ACTOR

★ **EDMUND GWENN—Miracle on 34th Street**
CHARLES BICKFORD—The Farmer's Daughter
THOMAS GOMEZ—Ride the Pink Horse
ROBERT RYAN—Crossfire
RICHARD WIDMARK—Kiss of Death

SUPPORTING ACTRESS

★ **CELESTE HOLM—Gentleman's Agreement**
ETHEL BARRYMORE—The Paradine Case
GLORIA GRAHAME—Crossfire
MARJORIE MAIN—The Egg and I
ANNE REVERE—Gentleman's Agreement

20th ACADEMY AWARDS   Hosted by Agnes Moorehead & Dick Powell

DIRECTOR

★ **GENTLEMAN'S AGREEMENT—Elia Kazan**
THE BISHOP'S WIFE—Henry Koster
CROSSFIRE—Edward Dmytryk
A DOUBLE LIFE—George Cukor
GREAT EXPECTATIONS—David Lean

CINEMATOGRAPHY (BLACK & WHITE)

★ **GREAT EXPECTATIONS—Guy Green**
THE GHOST AND MRS. MUIR—Charles Lang
GREEN DOLPHIN STREET—George Folsey

CINEMATOGRAPHY (COLOR)

★ **BLACK NARCISSUS—Jack Cardiff**
LIFE WITH FATHER—Peverell Marley & William V. Skall
MOTHER WORE TIGHTS—Harry Jackson

DRAMATIC SCORE

★ **A DOUBLE LIFE—Miklós Rózsa**
THE BISHOP'S WIFE—Hugo Friedhofer
CAPTAIN FROM CASTILE—Alfred Newman
FOREVER AMBER—David Raksin
LIFE WITH FATHER—Max Steiner

MUSICAL SCORE

★ **MOTHER WORE TIGHTS—Alfred Newman**
FIESTA—Johnny Green
MY WILD IRISH ROSE—Ray Heindorf and Max Steiner
ROAD TO REO—Robert Emmett Dolan
SONG OF THE SOUTH—Daniele Amfitheatrof, Paul J.
  Smith, Charles Wolcott

SONG

★ **ZIP-A-DEE-DOO-DAH** *from* **Song of the South**
A GAL IN CALICO *from* The Time, the Place, and the Girl
I WISH I DIDN'T LOVE YOU SO *from* The Perils of Pauline
PASS THAT PEACE PIPE *from* Good News
YOU DO *from* Mother Wore Tights

1949

BEST PICTURE

★ **HAMLET**
JOHNNY BELINDA
THE RED SHOES
THE SNAKE PIT
THE TREASURE OF THE SIERRA MADRE

ACTOR

★ **LAURENCE OLIVIER—Hamlet**
LEW AYRES—Johnny Belinda
MONTGOMERY CLIFT—The Search
DAN DAILEY—When My Baby Smiles at Me
CLIFTON WEBB—Sitting Pretty

ACTRESS

★ **JANE WYMAN—Johnny Belinda***
INGRID BERGMAN—Joan of Arc
OLIVIA de HAVILLAND—The Snake Pit
IRENE DUNNE—I Remember Mama
BARBARA STANWYCK—Sorry, Wrong Number

SUPPORTING ACTOR

★ **WALTER HUSTON—The Treasure of the Sierra Madre**
CHARLES BICKFORD—Johnny Belinda
JOSÉ FERRER—Joan of Arc
OSKAR HOMOLKA—I Remember Mama
CECIL KELLAWAY—The Luck of the Irish

SUPPORTING ACTRESS

★ **CLAIRE TREVOR—Key Largo**
BARBARA BEL GEDDES—I Remember Mama
ELLEN CORBY—I Remember Mama
AGNES MOOREHEAD—Johnny Belinda
JEAN SIMMONS—Hamlet

DIRECTOR

★ **THE TREASURE OF THE SIERRA MADRE—John Huston**
  HAMLET—Laurence Olivier
  JOHNNY BELINDA—Jean Negulesco
  THE SEARCH—Fred Zinnemann
  THE SNAKE PIT—Anatole Litvak

CINEMATOGRAPHY (BLACK & WHITE)

★ **THE NAKED CITY—William H. Daniels**
  A FOREIGN AFFAIR—Charles Lang
  I REMEMBER MAMA—Nicholas Musuraca
  JOHNNY BELINDA—Ted D. McCord
  PORTRAIT OF JENNIE—Joseph August

CINEMATOGRAPHY (COLOR)

★ **JOAN OF ARC—Joseph Valentine, William V. Skall, Winton Hoch**
  GREEN GRASS OF WYOMING—Charles G. Clarke
  THE LOVES OF CARMEN—William Snyder
  THE THREE MUSKETEERS—Robert Planck

DRAMATIC SCORE

★ **THE RED SHOES—Brian Easdale**
  HAMLET—William Walton
  JOAN OF ARC—Hugo Friedhofer
  JOHNNY BELINDA—Max Steiner
  THE SNAKE PIT—Alfred Newman

MUSICAL SCORE

★ **EASTER PARADE—Johnny Green and Roger Edens**
  THE EMPEROR WALTZ—Victor Young
  THE PIRATE—Lennie Hayton
  ROMANCE ON THE HIGH SEAS—Ray Heindorf
  WHEN MY BABY SMILES AT ME—Alfred Newman

SONG

★ **BUTTONS AND BOWS** *from* **The Paleface**
  FOR EVERY MAN THERE IS A WOMAN *from* Casbah
  IT'S MAGIC *from* Romance on the High Seas
  THIS IS THE MOMENT *from* That Lady in Ermine
  THE WOODY WOODPECKER SONG *from* Wet Blanket Policy

1950

New rule forbids pawning or selling Oscar statuettes.
(Academy will buy them back for one dollar.)

BEST PICTURE

★ **ALL THE KING'S MEN**
BATTLEGROUND
THE HEIRESS
A LETTER TO THREE WIVES
TWELVE O'CLOCK HIGH

ACTOR

★ **BRODERICK CRAWFORD—All the King's Men**
KIRK DOUGLAS—Champion
GREGORY PECK—Twelve O'Clock High
RICHARD TODD—The Hasty Heart
JOHN WAYNE—Sands of Iwo Jima

ACTRESS

★ **OLIVIA de HAVILLAND—The Heiress**
JEANNE CRAIN—Pinky
SUSAN HAYWARD—My Foolish Heart
DEBORAH KERR—Edward, My Son
LORETTA YOUNG—Come to the Stable

SUPPORTING ACTOR

★ **DEAN JAGGER—Twelve O'Clock High**
JOHN IRELAND—All the King's Men
ARTHUR KENNEDY—Champion
RALPH RICHARDSON—The Heiress
JAMES WHITMORE—Battleground

SUPPORTING ACTRESS

★ **MERCEDES McCAMBRIDGE—All the King's Men**
ETHEL BARRYMORE—Pinky
CELESTE HOLM—Come to the Stable
ELSA LANCHESTER—Come to the Stable
ETHEL WATERS—Pinky

DIRECTOR

★ **A LETTER TO THREE WIVES—Joseph L. Mankiewicz**
ALL THE KING'S MEN—Robert Rossen
BATTLEGROUND—William A. Wellman
THE FALLEN IDOL—Carol Reed
THE HEIRESS—William Wyler

CINEMATOGRAPHY (BLACK & WHITE)

★ **BATTLEGROUND—Paul C. Vogel**
CHAMPION—Franz—Planer
COME TO THE STABLE—Joseph LaShelle
THE HEIRESS—Leo Tover
PRINCE OF FOXES—Leon Shamroy

CINEMATOGRAPHY (COLOR)

★ **SHE WORE A YELLOW RIBBON—Winton Hoch**
THE BARKLEYS OF BROADWAY—Harry Stradling
JOLSON SINGS AGAIN—William Snyder
LITTLE WOMEN—Robert Planck & Charles Schoenbaum
SAND—Charles G. Clarke

DRAMATIC SCORE

★ **THE HEIRESS—Aaron Copland**
BEYOND THE FOREST—Max Steiner
CHAMPION—Dimitri Tiomkin

MUSICAL ADAPTATION

★ **ON THE TOWN—Roger Edens & Lennie Hayton**
JOLSON SINGS AGAIN—Morris Stoloff & George Duning
LOOK FOR THE SILVER LINING—Ray Heindorf

SONG

★ **BABY, IT'S COLD OUTSIDE** *from* **Neptune's Daughter**
IT'S A GREAT FEELING *from* It's a Great Feeling
LAVENDER BLUE *from* So Dear to My Heart
MY FOOLISH HEART *from* My Foolish Heart
THROUGH A LONG AND SLEEPLESS NIGHT *from*
Come to the Stable

1951

Marilyn Monroe steals every scene, including as presenter of EVE's Oscar for sound recording.

After 75 all-but-forgotten big screen roles, Lucille Ball steals TV limelight in I LOVE LUCY.

BEST PICTURE

★ **ALL ABOUT EVE***
BORN YESTERDAY
FATHER OF THE BRIDE
KING SOLOMON'S MINES
SUNSET BOULEVARD

ACTOR

★ **JOSÉ FERRER—Cyrano de Bergerac**
LOUIS CALHERN—The Magnificent Yankee
WILLIAM HOLDEN—Sunset Boulevard
JAMES STEWART—Harvey
SPENCER TRACY—Father of the Bride

ACTRESS

★ **JUDY HOLLIDAY—Born Yesterday**
ANNE BAXTER—All About Eve
BETTE DAVIS—All About Eve
ELEANOR PARKER—Caged
GLORIA SWANSON—Sunset Boulevard

SUPPORTING ACTOR

★ **GEORGE SANDERS—All About Eve**
JEFF CHANDLER—Broken Arrow
EDMUND GWENN—Mister 880
SAM JAFFE—The Asphalt Jungle
ERICH VON STROHEIM—Sunset Boulevard

SUPPORTING ACTRESS

★ **JOSEPHINE HULL—Harvey**
HOPE EMERSON—Caged
CELESTE HOLM—All About Eve
NANCY OLSON—Sunset Boulevard
THELMA RITTER—All About Eve

DIRECTOR

★ **ALL ABOUT EVE—Joseph L. Mankiewicz**
THE ASPHALT JUNGLE—John Huston
BORN YESTERDAY—George Cuker
SUNSET BOULEVARD—Billy Wilder
THE THIRD MAN—Carol Reed

CINEMATOGRAPHY (BLACK & WHITE)

★ **THE THIRD MAN—Robert Krasker**
ALL ABOUT EVE—Milton R. Krasner
THE ASPHALT JUNGLE—Harold Rosson
THE FURIES—Victor Milner
SUNSET BOULEVARD—John F. Seitz

CINEMATOGRAPHY (COLOR)

★ **KING SOLOMON'S MINES—Robert L. Surtees**
ANNIE GET YOUR GUN—Charles Rosher
BROKEN ARROW—Ernest Palmer
THE FLAME AND THE ARROW—Ernest Haller
SAMSON AND DELILAH—George Barnes

DRAMATIC SCORE

★ **SUNSET BOULEVARD—Franz Waxman**
ALL ABOUT EVE—Alfred Newman
THE FLAME AND THE ARROW—Max Steiner
NO SAD SONGS FOR ME—George Duning
SAMSON AND DELILAH—Victor Young

MUSICAL ADAPTATION

★ **ANNIE GET YOUR GUN—Adolph Deutsch & Roger Edens**
CINDERELLA—Oliver Wallace & Paul J. Smith
I'LL GET BY—Lionel Newman
THREE LITTLE WORDS—André Previn
THE WEST POINT STORY—Ray Heindorf

SONG

★ **MONA LISA** *from* **Captain Carey, U.S.A.**
BE MY LOVE *from* The Toast of New Orleans
BIBBIDI-BOBBIDI-BOO *from* Cinderella
MULE TRAIN *from* Singing Guns
WILHELMINA *from* Wabash Avenue

1952

Hononrary award goes to producer Merian C. Cooper, who, among other things, gave us KING KONG.

BEST PICTURE

★ **AN AMERICAN IN PARIS**
DECISION BEFORE DAWN
A PLACE IN THE SUN
QUO VADIS
A STREETCAR NAMED DESIRE

ACTOR

★ **HUMPHREY BOGART—The African Queen**
MARLON BRANDO—A Streetcar Named Desire
MONTGOMERY CLIFT—A Place in the Sun
ARTHUR KENNEDY—Bright Victory
FREDRIC MARCH—Death of a Salesman

ACTRESS

★ **VIVIEN LEIGH—A Streetcar Named Desire**
KATHARINE HEPBURN—The African Queen
ELEANOR PARKER—Detective Story
SHELLEY WINTERS—A Place in the Sun
JANE WYMAN—The Blue Veil

SUPPORTING ACTOR

★ **KARL MALDEN—A Streetcar Named Desire**
LEO GENN—Quo Vadis
KEVIN McCARTHY—Death of a Salesman
PETER USTINOV—Quo Vadis
GIG YOUNG—Come Fill the Cup

SUPPORTING ACTRESS

★ **KIM HUNTER—A Streetcar Named Desire**
JOAN BLONDELL—The Blue Veil
MILDRED DUNNOCK—Death of a Salesman
LEE GRANT—Detective Story
THELMA RITTER—The Mating Season

DIRECTOR

★ **A PLACE IN THE SUN—George Stevens**
THE AFRICAN QUEEN—John Huston
A STREETCAR NAMED DESIRE—Elia Kazan
AN AMERICAN IN PARIS—Vincente Minnelli
DETECTIVE STORY—William Wyler

CINEMATOGRAPHY (BLACK & WHITE)

★ **A PLACE IN THE SUN—William C. Mellor**
DEATH OF A SALESMAN—Franz Planer
THE FROGMEN—Norbert Brodine
STRANGERS ON A TRAIN—Robert Burks
A STREECAR NAMED DESIRE—Harry Stradling

CINEMATOGRAPHY (COLOR)

★ **AN AMERICAN IN PARIS—Alfred Gilks & John Alton**
DAVID AND BATHSHEBA—Leon Shamroy
QUO VADIS—Robert Surtees & William V. Scall SHOW BOAT—Charles Rosher
WHEN WORLDS COLLIDE—John F. Seitz & W. Howard Greene

DRAMATIC SCORE

★ **A PLACE IN THE SUN—Franz Waxman**
DAVID AND BATHSHEBA—Alfred Newman
DEATH OF A SALESMAN—Alex North
QUO VADIS—Miklós Rózsa
A STREETCAR NAMED DESIRE—Alex North

MUSICAL ADAPTATION

★ **AN AMERICAN IN PARIS—Johnny Green & Saul Chaplin**
ALICE IN WONDERLAND—Oliver Wallace
THE GREAT CARUSO—Peter Herman Adler & Johnny Green
ON THE RIVIERA—Alfred Newman
SHOW BOAT—Adolph Deutsch & Conrad Salinger

SONG

★ **IN THE COOL, COOL, COOL OF THE EVENING** *from* **Here Comes the Groom**
A KISS TO BUILD A DREAM ON *from* The Strip
NEVER *from* Golden Girl
TOO LATE NOW *from* Royal Wedding
WONDER WHY *from* Rich, Young, and Pretty

RKO Pantages Theater, Hollywood   March 20, 1952

1953

First televised Oscars.

BEST PICTURE

★ **THE GREATEST SHOW ON EARTH**
HIGH NOON
IVANHOE
MOULIN ROUGE
THE QUIET MAN

ACTOR

★ **GARY COOPER—High Noon**
MARLON BRANDO—Viva Zapata!
KIRK DOUGLAS—The Bad and the Beautiful
JOSÉ FERRER—Moulin Rouge
ALEC GUINNESS—The Lavender Hill Mob

ACTRESS

★ **SHIRLEY BOOTH—Come Back, Little Sheba**
JOAN CRAWFORD—Sudden Fear
BETTE DAVIS—The Star
JULIE HARRIS—The Member of the Wedding
SUSAN HAYWARD—With a Song in My Heart

SUPPORTING ACTOR

★ **ANTHONY QUINN—Viva Zapata!**
RICHARD BURTON—My Cousin Rachel
ARTHUR HUNNICUTT—The Big Sky
VICTOR McLAGLEN—The Quiet Man
JACK PALANCE—Sudden Fear

SUPPORTING ACTRESS

★ **GLORIA GRAHAME—The Bad and the Beautiful**
JEAN HAGEN—Singin' in the Rain
COLETTE MARCHAND—Moulin Rouge
TERRY MOORE—Come Back, Little Sheba
THELMA RITTER—With a Song in My Heart

DIRECTOR

★ **THE QUIET MAN—John Ford**
 FIVE FINGERS—Joseph L. Mankiewicz
 THE GREATEST SHOW ON EARTH—Cecil B. DeMille
 HIGH NOON—Fred Zinnemann
 MOULIN ROUGE—John Huston

CINEMATOGRAPHY (BLACK & WHITE)

★ **THE BAD AND THE BEAUTIFUL—Robert Surtees**
 THE BIG SKY—Russell Harlan
 MY COUSIN RACHEL—Joseph LaShelle
 NAVAJO—Virgil Miller
 SUDDEN FEAR—Charles Lang

CINEMATOGRAPHY (COLOR)

★ **THE QUIET MAN—Winton C. Hoch & Archie Stout**
 HANS CHRISTIAN ANDERSEN—Harry Stradling
 IVANHOE—F.A. Young
 MILLION DOLLAR MERMAID—George J. Folsey
 THE SNOWS OF KILIMANJARO—Leon Shamroy

DRAMATIC SCORE

★ **HIGH NOON—Dimitri Tiomkin**
 IVANHOE—Miklós Rózsa
 THE MIRACLE OF OUR LADY OF FATIMA—Max Steiner
 THE THIEF—Herschel Burke Gilbert
 VIVA ZAPATA!—Alex North

MUSICAL ADAPTATION

★ **WITH A SONG IN MY HEART—Alfred Newman**
 HANS CHRISTIAN ANDERSEN—Walter Scharf
 THE JAZZ SINGER—Ray Heindorf & Max Steiner
 THE MEDIUM—Gian-Carlo Menotti
 SINGIN' IN THE RAIN—Lennie Hayton

SONG

★ **DO NOT FORSAKE ME, O MY DARLIN'** *from* **High Noon**
 AM I IN LOVE *from* Son of Paleface
 BECAUSE YOUR MINE *from* Because Your Mine
 THUMBELINA *from* Hans Christian Andersen
 ZING A LITTLE ZONG *from* Just for You

1954

Godzilla makes debut in Japanese film Gorira.

BEST PICTURE

★ **FROM HERE TO ETERNITY**
JULIUS CAESAR
THE ROBE
ROMAN HOLIDAY
SHANE

ACTOR

★ **WILLIAM HOLDEN—Stalag 17**
MARLON BRANDO—Julius Caesar
RICHARD BURTON—The Robe
MONTGOMERY CLIFT—From Here to Eternity
BURT LANCASTER—From Here to Eternity

ACTRESS

★ **AUDREY HEPBURN—Roman Holiday**
LESLIE CARON—Lili
AVA GARDNER—Mogambo
DEBORAH KERR—From Here to Eternity
MAGGIE McNAMARA—The Moon is Blue

SUPPORTING ACTOR

★ **FRANK SINATRA—From Here to Eternity**
EDDIE ALBERT—Roman Holiday
BRANDON de WILDE—Shane
JACK PALANCE—Shane
ROBERT STRAUSS—Stalag 17

SUPPORTING ACTRESS

★ **DONNA REED—From Here to Eternity**
GRACE KELLY—Mogambo
GERALDINE PAGE—Hondo
MARJORIE RAMBEAU—Torch Song
THELMA RITTER—Pickup on South Street

DIRECTOR

★ **FROM HERE TO ETERNITY—Fred Zinnemann**
LILI—Charles Walters
ROMAN HOLIDAY—William Wyler
SHANE—George Stevens
STALAG 17—Billy Wilder

CINEMATOGRAPHY (BLACK & WHITE)

★ **FROM HERE TO ETERNITY—Burnett Guffey**
THE FOUR POSTER—Hal Mohr
JULIUS CAESAR—Joseph Ruttenberg
MARTIN LUTHER—Joseph C. Brun
ROMAN HOLIDAY—Franz Planer & Henri Alekan

CINEMATOGRAPHY (COLOR)

★ **SHANE—Loyal Griggs**
ALL THE BROTHERS WERE VALIANT—George Folsey
BENEATH THE 12-MILE REEF—Edward Cronjager
LILI—Robert Planck
THE ROBE—Leon Shamroy

DRAMATIC SCORE

★ **LILI—Bronislau Kaper**
ABOVE AND BEYOND—Hugo Friedhofer
FROM HERE TO ETERNITY—Morris Stoloff and
    George Duning
JULIUS CAESAR—Miklós Rózsa
THIS IS CINERAMA—Louis Forbes

MUSICAL ADAPTATION

★ **CALL ME MADAM—Alfred Newman**
THE 5,000 FINGERS OF DR. T—Frederick Hollander and
    Morris Stoloff
THE BAND WAGON—Adolph Deutsch
CALAMITY JANE—Ray Heindorf
KISS ME KATE—André Previn and Saul Chaplin

SONG

★ **SECRET LOVE** *from* **Calamity Jane**
THE MOON IS BLUE *from* The Moon is Blue
MY FLAMING HEART *from* Small Town Girl
SADIE THOMPSON'S SONG *from* Miss Sadie Thompson
THAT'S AMORE *from* The Caddy

1955

Disneyland opens.

BEST PICTURE

★ **ON THE WATERFRONT**
THE CAINE MUTINY
THE COUNTRY GIRL
SEVEN BRIDES FOR SEVEN BROTHERS
THREE COINS IN THE FOUNTAIN

ACTOR

★ **MARLON BRANDO—On the Waterfront**
HUMPHREY BOGART—The Caine Mutiny
BING CROSBY—The Country Girl
JAMES MASON—A Star is Born
DAN O'HERLIHY—Robinson Crusoe

ACTRESS

★ **GRACE KELLY—The Country Girl**
DOROTHY DANDRIDGE—Carmen Jones
JUDY GARLAND—A Star Is Born
AUDREY HEPBURN—Sabrina
JANE WYMAN—Magnificent Obsession

SUPPORTING ACTOR

★ **EDMOND O'BRIEN—The Barefoot Contessa**
LEE J. COBB—On the Waterfront
KARL MALDEN—On the Waterfront
ROD STEIGER—On the Waterfront
TOM TULLY—The Caine Mutiny

SUPPORTING ACTRESS

★ **EVA MARIE SAINT—On the Waterfront**
NINA FOCH—Executive Suite
KATY JURADO—Broken Lance
JAN STERLING—The High and the Mighty
CLAIRE TREVOR—The High and the Mighty

DIRECTOR

★ **ON THE WATERFRONT—Elia Kazan**
THE COUNTRY GIRL—George Seaton
THE HIGH AND THE MIGHTY—William A. Welllman
REAR WINDOW—Alfred Hitchcock
SABRINA—Billy Wilder

CINEMATOGRAPHY (BLACK & WHITE)

★ **ON THE WATERFRONT—Boris Kaufman**
THE COUNTRY GIRL—John F. Warren
EXECUTIVE SUITE—George Folsey
ROGUE COP—John Seitz
SABRINA—Charles Lang

CINEMATOGRAPHY (COLOR)

★ **THREE COINS IN THE FOUNTAIN—Milton Krasner**
THE EGYPTIAN—Leon Shamroy
REAR WINDOW—Robert Burks
SEVEN BRIDES FOR SEVEN BROTHERS—George Folsey
THE SILVER CHALICE—William V. Skall

DRAMATIC SCORE

★ **THE HIGH AND THE MIGHTY—Dimitri Tiomkin**
THE CAINE MUTINY—Max Steiner
GENEVIEVE—Larry Adler
ON THE WATERFRONT—Leonard Bernstein
THE SILVER CHALICE—Franz Waxman

MUSICAL ADAPTATION

★ **SEVEN BRIDES FOR SEVEN BROTHERS—Adolph Deutsch and Saul Chaplin**
CARMEN JONES—Herschel Burke Gilbert
THE GLENN MILLER STORY—Joseph Gershenson & Henry Mancini
A STAR IS BORN—Ray Heindorf
THERE'S NO BUSINESS LIKE SHOW BUSINESS—Alfred Newman and Lionel Newman

SONG

★ **THREE COINS IN THE FOUNTAIN** *from* **Three Coins in the Fountain**
COUNT YOUR BLESSINGS INSTEAD OF SHEEP from White Christmas
THE HIGH AND THE MIGHTY *from* The High and the Mighty
HOLD MY HAND *from* Susan Slept Here
THE MAN THAT GOT AWAY *from* A Star is Born

1956

Killed in car crash, Dean gets posthumous nomination.

BEST PICTURE

★ **MARTY**
LOVE IS A MANY-SPLENDORED THING
MISTER ROBERTS
PICNIC
THE ROSE TATTOO

ACTOR

★ **ERNEST BORGNINE—Marty**
JAMES CAGNEY—Love Me or Leave Me
JAMES DEAN—East of Eden*
FRANK SINATRA—The Man with the Golden Arm
SPENCER TRACY—Bad Day at Black Rock

ACTRESS

★ **ANNA MAGNANI—The Rose Tattoo**
SUSAN HAYWARD—I'll Cry Tomorrow
KATHARINE HEPBURN—Summertime
JENNIFER JONES—Love Is a Many-Splendored Thing
ELEANOR PARKER—Interrupted Melody

SUPPORTING ACTOR

★ **JACK LEMMON—Mr. Roberts**
ARTHUR KENNEDY—Trial
JOE MANTELL—Marty
SAL MINEO—Rebel Without a Cause
ARTHUR O'CONNELL—Picnic

SUPPORTING ACTRESS

★ **JO VAN FLEET—East of Eden**
BETSY BLAIR—Marty
PEGGY LEE—Pete Kelly's Blues
MARISA PAVAN—The Rose Tattoo
NATALIE WOOD—Rebel Without a Cause

DIRECTOR

★ **MARTY—Delbert Mann**
BAD DAY AT BLACK ROCK—John Sturges
EAST OF EDEN—Elia Kazan
PICNIC—Joshua Logan
SUMMERTIME—David Lean

CINEMATOGRAPHY (BLACK & WHITE)

★ **THE ROSE TATTOO—James Wong Howe**
BLACKBOARD JUNGLE—Russell Harlan
I'LL CRY TOMORROW—Arthur E. Arling
MARTY—Joseph LaShelle
QUEEN BEE—Charles Lang

CINEMATOGRAPHY (COLOR)

★ **TO CATCH A THIEF—Robert Burks**
GUYS AND DOLLS—Harry Stradling
LOVE IS A MANY-SPLENDORED THING—Leon Shamroy
A MAN CALLED PETER—Harold Lipstein
OKLAHOMA!—Robert Surtees

DRAMATIC SCORE

★ **LOVE IS A MANY-SPLENDORED THING—Alfred Newman**
BATTLE CRY—Max Steiner
THE MAN WITH THE GOLDEN ARM—Elmer Bernstein
PICNIC—George Duning
THE ROSE TATTOO—Alex North

MUSICAL ADAPTATION

★ **OKLAHOMA!—Robert Russell Bennett, Jay Blackton, Adolph Deutsch**
DADDY LONG LEGS—Alfred Newman
GUYS AND DOLLS—Jay Blackton and Cyril J. Mockridge
IT'S ALWAYS FAIR WEATHER—André Previn
LOVE ME OR LEAVE ME—Percy Faith and George Stoll

SONG

★ **LOVE IS A MANY-SPLENDORED THING** *from* **Love is a Many-Splendored Thing**
I'LL NEVER STOP LOVING YOU from Love Me or Leave Me
SOMETHING'S GOTTA GIVE *from* Daddy Long Legs
THE TENDER TRAP *from* The Tender Trap
UNCHAINED MELODY *from* Unchained

1957

Foreign Language Film category introduced.

BEST PICTURE

★ **AROUND THE WORLD IN EIGHTY DAYS**
FRIENDLY PERSUASION
GIANT
THE KING AND I
THE TEN COMMANDMENTS

ACTOR

★ **YUL BRYNNER—The King and I**
JAMES DEAN—Giant
KIRK DOUGLAS—Lust for Life
ROCK HUDSON—Giant
LAURENCE OLIVIER—Richard III

ACTRESS

★ **INGRID BERGMAN—Anastasia**
CARROLL BAKER—Baby Doll
KATHARINE HEPBURN—The Rainmaker
NANCY KELLY—The Bad Seed
DEBORAH KERR—The King and I

SUPPORTING ACTOR

★ **ANTHONY QUINN—Lust for Life**
DON MURRAY—Bus Stop
ANTHONY PERKINS—Friendly Persuasion
MICKEY ROONEY—The Bold and the Brave
ROBERT STACK—Written on the Wind

SUPPORTING ACTRESS

★ **DOROTHY MALONE—Written on the Wind**
MILDRED DUNNOCK—Baby Doll
EILEEN HECKART—The Bad Seed
MERCEDES McCAMBRIDGE—Giant
PATTY McCORMACK—The Bad Seed

DIRECTOR

★ **GIANT—George Stevens**
AROUND THE WORLD IN 80 DAYS—Michael Anderson
FRIENDLY PERSUASION—William Wyler
THE KING AND I—Walter Lang
WAR AND PEACE—King Vidor

CINEMATOGRAPHY (BLACK & WHITE)

★ **SOMEBODY UP THERE LIKES ME—Joseph Ruttenberg**
BABY DOLL—Boris Kaufman
THE BAD SEED—Harold Rosson
THE HARDER THEY FALL—Burnett Guffey
STAGECOACH TO FURY—Walter Strenge

CINEMATOGRAPHY (COLOR)

★ **AROUND THE WORLD IN 80 DAYS—Lionel Lindon**
THE EDDY DUCHIN STORY—Harry Stradling
THE KING AND I—Leon Shamroy
THE TEN COMMANDMENTS—Loyal Griggs
WAR AND PEACE—Jack Cardiff

DRAMATIC SCORE

★ **AROUND THE WORLD IN 80 DAYS—Victor Young**
ANASTASIA—Alfred Newman
BETWEEN HEAVEN AND HELL—Hugo Friedhofer
GIANT—Dmitri Tiomkin
THE RAINMAKER—Alex North

MUSICAL ADAPTATION

★ **THE KING AND I—Alfred Newman & Ken Darby**
THE BEST THINGS IN LIFE ARE FREE—Lionel Newman
THE EDDIE DUCHIN STORY—Morris Stoloff & George Duning
HIGH SOCIETY—Johnny Green and Saul Chaplin
MEET ME IN LAS VEGAS—George Stoll and Johnny Green

SONG

★ **QUE SERA, SERA** *from* **The Man Who Knew Too Much**
FRIENDLY PERSUASION (Thee I Love) from Friendly Persuasion
JULIE *from* Julie
TRUE LOVE *from* High Society
WRITTEN ON THE WIND *from* Written on the Wind

1958

BEST PICTURE

★ **THE BRIDGE ON THE RIVER KWAI***
12 ANGRY MEN
PEYTON PLACE
SAYONARA
WITNESS FOR THE PROSECUTION

ACTOR

★ **ALEC GUINNESS—The Bridge on the River Kwai**
MARLON BRANDO—Sayonara
ANTHONY FRANCIOSA—A Hatful of Rain
CHARLES LAUGHTON—Witness for the Prosecution
ANTHONY QUINN—Wild is the Wind

ACTRESS

★ **JOANNE WOODWARD—The Three Faces of Eve**
DEBORAH KERR—Heaven Knows, Mr. Allison
ANNA MAGNANI—Wild is the Wind
ELIZABETH TAYLOR—Raintree County
LANA TURNER—Peyton Place

SUPPORTING ACTOR

★ **RED BUTTONS—Sayonara**
VITTORIO DE SICA—A Farewell to Arms
SESSUE HAYAKAWA—The Bridge on the River Kwai
ARTHUR KENNEDY—Peyton Place
RUSS TAMBLYN—Peyton Place

SUPPORTING ACTRESS

★ **MIYOSHI UMEKI—Sayonara**
CAROLYN JONES—The Bachelor Party
ELSA LANCHESTER—Witness for the Prosecution
HOPE LANGE—Peyton Place
DIANE VARSI—Peyton Place

DIRECTOR

★ **THE BRIDGE ON THE RIVER KWAI—David Lean**
   12 ANGRY MEN—Sidney Lumet
   PEYTON PLACE—Mark Robson
   SAYONARA—Joshua Logan
   WITNESS FOR THE PROSECUTION—Billy Wilder

CINEMATOGRAPHY

★ **THE BRIDGE ON THE RIVER KWAI—Jack Hildyard**
   AN AFFAIR TO REMEMBER—Milton Krasner
   FUNNY FACE—Ray June
   PEYTON PLACE—William C. Mellor
   SAYONARA—Ellsworth Fredericks

SCREENPLAY ADAPTATION

★ **THE BRIDGE ON THE RIVER KWAI—*from the novel****
   12 ANGRY MEN—*from the teleplay*
   HEAVEN KNOWS, MR. ALLISON—*from the novel*
   PEYTON PLACE—*from the novel*
   SAYONARA—*from the novel*

VISUAL EFFECTS

★ **THE ENEMY BELOW**
   THE SPIRIT OF ST. LOUIS

SCORE

★ **THE BRIDGE ON THE RIVER KWAI—Malcolm Arnold**
   AN AFFAIR TO REMEMBER—Hugo Friedhofer
   BOY ON A DOLPHIN—Hugo Friedhofer
   PERRI—Paul J. Smith
   RAINTRE COUNTY—Johnny Green

SONG

★ **ALL THE WAY** *from* **The Joker is Wild**
   AN AFFAIR TO REMEMBER *from* An Affair to Remember
   APRIL LOVE *from* April Love
   TAMMY *from* Tammy and the Bachelor
   WILD IS THE WIND *from* Wild is the Wind

1959

Too many edits produce shortest Oscar show on record;
*Jerry Lewis struggles to fill 20 leftover minutes.

BEST PICTURE

★ **GIGI**
AUNTIE MAME
CAT ON A HOT TIN ROOF
THE DEFIANT ONES
SEPARATE TABLES

ACTOR

★ **DAVID NIVEN—Separate Tables**
TONY CURTIS—The Defiant Ones
PAUL NEWMAN—Cat on a Hot Tin Roof
SIDNEY POITIER—The Defiant Ones
SPENCER TRACY—The Old Man and the Sea

ACTRESS

★ **SUSAN HAYWARD—I Want to Live!**
DEBORAH KERR—Separate Tables
SHIRLEY MacLAINE—Some Came Running
ROSALIND RUSSELL—Auntie Mame
ELIZABETH TAYLOR—Cat on a Hot Tin Roof

SUPPORTING ACTOR

★ **BURL IVES—The Big Country**
THEODORE BIKEL—The Defiant Ones
LEE J. COBB—The Brothers Karamazov
ARTHUR KENNEDY—Some Came Running
GIG YOUNG—Teacher's Pet

SUPPORTING ACTRESS

★ **WENDY HILLER—Separate Tables**
PEGGY CASS—Auntie Mame
MARTHA HYER—Some Came Running
MAUREEN STAPLETON—Lonelyhearts
CARA WILLIAMS—The Defiant Ones

DIRECTOR

★ **GIGI—Vincente Minnelli**
CAT ON A HOT TIN ROOF—Richard Brooks
THE DEFIANT ONES—Stanley Kramer
I WANT TO LIVE!—Robert Wise
THE INN OF THE SIXTH HAPPINESS—Mark Robson

CINEMATOGRAPHY (BLACK & WHITE)

★ **THE DEFIANT ONES—Sam Leavitt**
DESIRE UNDER THE ELMS—Daniel L. Fapp
I WANT TO LIVE!—Lionel Lindon
SEPARATE TABLES—Charles Lang Jr.
THE YOUNG LIONS—Joseph MacDonald

CINEMATOGRAPHY (COLOR)

★ **GIGI—Joseph Ruttenberg**
AUNTIE MAME—Harry Stradling
CAT ON A HOT TIN ROOF—William Daniels
THE OLD MAN AND THE SEA—James Wong Howe
SOUTH PACIFIC—Leon Shamroy

DRAMATIC SCORE

★ **THE OLD MAN AND THE SEA—Dimitri Tiomkin**
THE BIG COUNTRY—Jerome Moross
SEPARATE TABLES—David Raksin
WHITE WILDERNESS—Oliver Wallace
THE YOUNG LIONS—Hugo Friedhofer

MUSICAL ADAPTATION

★ **GIGI—André Previn**
THE BOLSHOI BALLET—Yuri Faier & G. Rozhdestvensky
DAMN YANKEES!—Ray Heindorf
MARDI GRAS—Lionel Newman
SOUTH PACIFIC—Alfred Newman and Ken Darby

SONG

★ **GIGI** *from* **Gigi**
A CERTAIN SMILE *from* A Certain Smile
ALMOST IN YOUR ARMS *from* Houseboat
TO LOVE AND BE LOVED *from* Some Came Running
A VERY PRECIOUS LOVE *from* Marjorie Morningstar

1960

*PSYCHO draws lines around block,
but few nods for '61 noms.*

BEST PICTURE

★ **BEN-HUR**
ANATOMY OF A MURDER
THE DIARY OF ANNE FRANK
THE NUN'S STORY
ROOM AT THE TOP

ACTOR

★ **CHARLTON HESTON—Ben-Hur**
LAURENCE HARVEY—Room at the Top
JACK LEMMON—Some Like it Hot
PAUL MUNI—The Last Angry Man
JAMES STEWART—Anatomy of a Murder

ACTRESS

★ **SIMONE SIGNORET—Room at the Top**
DORIS DAY—Pillow Talk
AUDREY HEPBURN—The Nun's Story
KATHARINE HEPBURN—Suddenly, Last Summer
ELIZABETH TAYLOR—Suddenly, Last Summer

SUPPORTING ACTOR

★ **HUGH GRIFFITH—Ben-Hur**
ARTHUR O'CONNELL—Anatomy of a Murder
GEORGE C. SCOTT—Anatomy of a Murder
ROBERT VAUGHN—The Young Philadelphians
ED WYNN—The Diary of Anne Frank

SUPPORTING ACTRESS

★ **SHELLEY WINTERS—The Diary of Anne Frank**
HERMIONE BADDELEY—Room at the Top
SUSAN KOHNER—Imitation of Life
JUANITA MOORE—Imitation of Life
THELMA RITTER—Pillow Talk

DIRECTOR

★ **BEN HUR—William Wyler**
THE DIARY OF ANNE FRANK—George Stevens
THE NUN'S STORY—Fred Zinneman
ROOM AT THE TOP—Jack Clayton
SOME LIKE IT HOT—Billy Wilder

CINEMATOGRAPHY (BLACK & WHITE)

★ **THE DIARY OF ANNE FRANK—William C. Mellor**
ANATOMY OF A MURDER—Sam Leavitt
CAREER—Joseph LaShelle
SOME LIKE IT HOT—Charles Lang Jr.
THE YOUNG PHILADELPHIANS—Harry Stradling

CINEMATOGRAPHY (COLOR)

★ **BEN-HUR—Robert L. Surtees**
THE BIG FISHERMAN—Lee Garmes
THE FIVE PENNIES—Daniel L. Fapp
THE NUN'S STORY—Franz Planer
PORGY AND BESS—Leon Shamroy

DRAMATIC SCORE

★ **BEN-HUR—Miklós Rózsa**
THE DIARY OF ANNE FRANK—Alfred Newman
THE NUN'S STORY—Franz Waxman
ON THE BEACH—Ernest Gold
PILLOW TALK—Frank DeVol

MUSICAL ADAPTATION

★ **PORGY AND BESS—André Previn and Ken Darby**
THE FIVE PENNIES—Leith Stevens
L'IL ABNER—Nelson Riddle and Joseph J. Lilley
SAY ONE FOR ME—Lionel Newman
SLEEPING BEAUTY—George Bruns

SONG

★ **HIGH HOPES** *from* **A Hole in the Head**
THE BEST OF EVERYTHING *from* The Best of Everything
THE FIVE PENNIES *from* The Five Pennies
THE HANGING TREE *from* The Hanging Tree
STRANGE ARE THE WAYS OF LOVE *from* The Young Land

1961

Shortest Speech—Wilder:
"Thank you so much, you lovely discerning people."

BEST PICTURE

★ **THE APARTMENT**
THE ALAMO
ELMER GANTRY
SONS AND LOVERS
THE SUNDOWNERS

ACTOR

★ **BURT LANCASTER—Elmer Gantry**
TREVOR HOWARD—Sons and Lovers
JACK LEMMON—The Apartment
LAURENCE OLIVIER—The Entertainer
SPENCER TRACY—Inherit the Wind

ACTRESS

★ **ELIZABETH TAYLOR—Butterfield 8**
GREER GARSON—Sunrise at Campobello
DEBORAH KERR—The Sundowners
SHIRLEY MacLAINE—The Apartment
MELINA MERCOURI—Never on Sunday

SUPPORTING ACTOR

★ **PETER USTINOV—Spartacus**
PETER FALK—Murder, Inc.
JACK KRUSCHEN—The Apartment
SAL MINEO—Exodus
CHILL WILLS—The Alamo

SUPPORTING ACTRESS

★ **SHIRLEY JONES—Elmer Gantry**
GLYNIS JOHNS—The Sundowners
SHIRLEY KNIGHT—The Dark at the Top of the Stairs
JANET LEIGH—Psycho
MARY URE—Sons and Lovers

DIRECTOR

★ **THE APARTMENT—Billy Wilder***
NEVER ON SUNDAY—Jules Dassin
PSYCHO—Alfred Hitchcock
SONS AND LOVERS—Jack Cardiff
THE SUNDOWNERS—Fred Zinnemann

CINEMATOGRAPHY (BLACK & WHITE)

★ **SONS AND LOVERS—Freddie Francis**
THE APARTMENT—Joseph LaShelle
THE FACTS OF LIFE—Charles Lang Jr.
INHERIT THE WIND—Ernest Laszlo
PSYCHO—John L. Russell

CINEMATOGRAPHY (COLOR)

★ **SPARTACUS—Russell Metty**
THE ALAMO—William H. Clothier
BUTTERFIELD 8—Joseph Ruttenberg & Charles Harten
EXODUS—Sam Leavitt
PEPE—Joseph MacDonald

DRAMATIC SCORE

★ **EXODUS—Ernest Gold**
THE ALAMO—Dimitri Tiomkin
ELMER GANTRY—André Previn
THE MAGNIFICENT SEVEN—Elmer Bernstein
SPARTACUS—Alex North

MUSICAL ADAPTATION

★ **SONG WITHOUT END—Morris Stoloff & Harry Sukman**
BELLS ARE RINGING—André Previn
CAN-CAN—Nelson Riddle
LET'S MAKE LOVE—Lionel Newman & Earle H. Hagen
PEPE—Johnny Green

SONG

★ **NEVER ON SUNDAY** *from* **Never on Sunday**
THE FACTS OF LIFE *from* The Facts of Life
FARAWAY PART OF TOWN *from* PEPE
THE GREEN LEAVES OF SUMMER *from* THE ALAMO
THE SECOND TIME AROUND *from* HIGH TIME

1962

Shortest Speech--Moreno:
"I can't believe it!! ... I'll just leave you with that."

BEST PICTURE

★ **WEST SIDE STORY**
FANNY
THE GUNS OF NAVARONE
THE HUSTLER
JUDGMENT AT NUREMBERG

ACTOR

★ **MAXIMILIAN SCHELL—Judgment at Nuremberg**
CHARLES BOYER—Fanny
PAUL NEWMAN—The Hustler
SPENCER TRACY—Judgment at Nuremberg
STUART WHITMAN—The Mark

ACTRESS

★ **SOPHIA LOREN—Two Women**
AUDREY HEPBURN—Breakfast at Tiffany's
PIPER LAURIE—The Hustler
GERALDINE PAGE—Summer and Smoke
NATALIE WOOD—Splendor in the Grass

SUPPORTING ACTOR

★ **GEORGE CHAKIRIS—West Side Story**
MONTGOMERY CLIFT—Judgment at Nuremberg
PETER FALK—Pocketful of Miracles
JACKIE GLEASON—The Hustler
GEORGE C. SCOTT—The Hustler

SUPPORTING ACTRESS

★ **RITA MORENO—West Side Story***
FAY BAINTER—The Children's Hour
JUDY GARLAND—Judgment at Nuremberg
LOTTE LENYA—The Roman Spring of Mrs. Stone
UNA MERKEL—Summer and Smoke

DIRECTOR

★ **WEST SIDE STORY—Robert Wise & Jerome Robbins**
LA DOLCE VITA—Federico Fellini
THE GUNS OF NAVARONE—J. Lee Thompson
THE HUSTLER—Robert Rossen
JUDGMENT AT NUREMBERG—Stanley Kramer

CINEMATOGRAPHY (BLACK & WHITE)

★ **THE HUSTLER—Eugen Schüfftan**
THE ABSENT-MINDED PROFESSOR—Edward Colman
THE CHILDREN'S HOUR—Franz Planer
JUDGMENT AT NUREMBERG—Ernest Laszlo
ONE, TWO, THREE—Daniel L. Fapp

CINEMATOGRAPHY (COLOR)

★ **WEST SIDE STORY—Daniel L. Fapp**
FANNY—Jack Cardiff
FLOWER DRUM SONG—Russell Metty
A MAJORITY OF ONE—Harry Stradling
ONE-EYED JACKS—Charles Lang Jr.

DRAMATIC SCORE

★ **BREAKFAST AT TIFFANY'S—Henry Mancini**
EL CID—Miklós Rózsa
FANNY—Morris Stoloff and Harry Sukman
THE GUNS OF NAVARONE—Dimitri Tiomkin SUMMER AND SMOKE—Elmer Bernstein

MUSICAL ADAPTATION

★ **WEST SIDE STORY—Saul Chaplin, Johnny Green, Sid Ramin, Irwin Kostal**
BABES IN TOYLAND—George Bruns
FLOWER DRUM SONG—Alfred Newman, Ken Darby
KHOVANSHCHINA—Dmitri Shostakovich
PARIS BLUES—Duke Ellington

SONG

★ **MOON RIVER** *from* **Breakfast at Tiffany's**
BACHELOR IN PARADISE *from* Bachelor in Paradise
THE FALCON AND THE DOVE *from* El Cid
POCKETFUL OF MIRACLES *from* Pocketful of Miracles
TOWN WITHOUT PITY *from* Town without Pity

1963

BEST PICTURE

★ **LAWRENCE OF ARABIA**
  THE LONGEST DAY
  THE MUSIC MAN
  MUTINY ON THE BOUNTY
  TO KILL A MOCKINGBIRD

ACTOR

★ **GREGORY PECK—To Kill a Mockingbird**
  BURT LANCASTER—Birdman of Alcatraz
  JACK LEMMON—Days of Wine and Roses
  MARCELLO MASTROIANNI—Divorce Italian Style
  PETER O'TOOLE—Lawrence of Arabia

ACTRESS

★ **ANNE BANCROFT—The Miracle Worker***
  BETTE DAVIS—What Ever Happened to Baby Jane?*
  KATHARINE HEPBURN—Long Day's Journey into Night
  GERALDINE PAGE—Sweet Bird of Youth
  LEE REMICK—Days of Wine and Roses

SUPPORTING ACTOR

★ **ED BEGLEY—Sweet Bird of Youth**
  VICTOR BUONO—What Ever Happened to Baby Jane?
  TELLY SAVALAS—Birdman of Alcatraz
  OMAR SHARIF—Lawrence of Arabia
  TERENCE STAMP—Billy Budd

SUPPORTING ACTRESS

★ **PATTY DUKE—The Miracle Worker**
  MARY BADHAM—To Kill a Mockingbird
  SHIRLEY KNIGHT—Sweet Bird of Youth
  ANGELA LANSBURY—The Manchurian Candidate
  THELMA RITTER—Birdman of Alcatraz

DIRECTOR

★ **LAWRENCE OF ARABIA—David Lean**
DAVID AND LISA—Frank Perry
DIVORCE ITALIAN STYLE—Pietro Germi
THE MIRACLE WORKER—Arthur Penn
TO KILL A MOCKINGBIRD—Robert Mulligan

CINEMATOGRAPHY (BLACK & WHITE)

★ **THE LONGEST DAY—Jean Bourgoin and Walter Wottitz**
BIRDMAN OF ALCATRAZ—Burnett Guffey
TO KILL A MOCKINGBIRD—Russell Harlan
TWO FOR THE SEESAW—Ted D. McCord
WHAT EVER HAPPENED TO BABY JANE?—Ernest Haller

CINEMATOGRAPHY (COLOR)

★ **LAWRENCE OF ARABIA—Freddie Young**
GYPSY—Harry Stradling
HATARI!—Russell Harlan
MUTINY ON THE BOUNTY—Robert Surtees
THE WONDERFUL WORLD OF THE BROTHERS GRIMM
—Paul C. Vogel

DRAMATIC SCORE

★ **LAWRENCE OF ARABIA—Maurice Jarre**
FREUD—Jerry Goldsmith
MUTINY ON THE BOUNTY—Bronislau Kaper
TARAS BULBA—Franz Waxman
TO KILL A MOCKINGBIRD—Elmer Bernstein

MUSICAL ADAPTATION

★ **THE MUSIC MAN—Ray Heindorf**
BILLY ROSE'S JUMBO—George Stoll
GIGOT—Michel Magne
GYPSY—Frank Perkins
THE WONDERFUL WORLD OF THE BROTHERS GRIMM
—Leigh Harline

SONG

★ **DAYS OF WINE AND ROSES** *from* **Days of Wine and Roses**
FOLLOW ME *from* Mutiny on the Bounty
SECOND CHANCE *from* Two for the Seesaw
TENDER IS THE NIGHT *from* Tender is the Night
WALK ON THE WILD SIDE *from* Walk on the Wild Side

1964

*First Black male actor leading role winner;
Hattie McDaniel only previous Black winner (supporting role GWTW).*

BEST PICTURE

★ **TOM JONES**
   AMERICA AMERICA
   CLEOPATRA
   HOW THE WEST WAS WON
   LILIES OF THE FIELD

ACTOR

★ **SIDNEY POITIER—Lilies of the Field***
   ALBERT FINNEY—Tom Jones
   RICHARD HARRIS—This Sporting Life
   REX HARRISON--Cleopatra
   PAUL NEWMAN—Hud

ACTRESS

★ **PATRICIA NEAL—Hud**
   LESLIE CARON—The L-Shaped Room
   SHIRLEY MacLAINE—Irma La Douce
   RACHEL ROBERTS—This Sporting Life
   NATALIE WOOD—Love with the Proper Stranger

SUPPORTING ACTOR

★ **MELVYN DOUGLAS—Hud**
   NICK ADAMS—Twilight of Honor
   BOBBY DARIN—Captain Newman, M.D.
   HUGH GRIFFITH—Tom Jones
   JOHN HUSTON—The Cardinal

SUPPORTING ACTRESS

★ **MARGARET RUTHERFORD—The V.I.P.s**
   DIANE CILENTO—Tom Jones
   EDITH EVANS—Tom Jones
   JOYCE REDMAN—Tom Jones
   LILIA SKALA—Lilies of the Field

DIRECTOR

★ **TOM JONES—Tony Richardson**
8½—Federico Fellini
AMERICA AMERICA—Elia Kazan
THE CARDINAL—Otto Preminger
HUD—Martin Ritt

CINEMATOGRAPHY (BLACK & WHITE)

★ **HUD-James Wong Howe**
THE BALCONY—George Folsey
THE CARETAKERS—Lucien Ballard
LILIES OF THE FIELD—Ernest Haller
LOVE WITH THE PROPER STRANGER—Milton Krasner

CINEMATOGRAPHY (COLOR)

★ **CLEOPATRA—Leon Shamroy**
THE CARDINAL—Leon Shamroy
HOW THE WEST WAS WON—William Daniels, Milton
    Krasner, Charles Lang Jr., Joseph LaShelle
IRMA LA DOUCE—Joseph LaShelle
IT'S A MAD, MAD, MAD, MAD WORLD—Ernest Laszki

ORIGINAL SCORE

★ **TOM JONES—John Addison**
55 DAYS AT PEKING—Dimitri Tiomkin
CLEOPATRA—Alex North
HOW THE WEST WAS WON—Alfred Newman & Ken Darby
IT'S A MAD, MAD, MAD, MAD WORLD—Ernest Gold

MUSICAL ADAPTATION

★ **IRMA LA DOUCE—André Previn**
BYE BYE BIRDIE—Johnny Green
A NEW KIND OF LOVE—Leith Stevens
SUNDAYS AND CYBELE—Maurice Jarre
THE SWORD IN THE STONE—George Bruns

SONG

★ **CALL ME IRRESPONSIBLE** *from* **Papa's Delicate
    Condition**
CHARADE *from* Charade
IT'S A MAD, MAD, MAD, MAD WORLD *from* It's a Mad,
    Mad, Mad, Mad World
MORE *from* Mondo Cane
SO LITTLE TIME *from* 55 Days at Peking

1965

In Golden Globe speech, Broadway's Fair Lady gives back-handed thanks to Jack Warner, who past her over for film role.

BEST PICTURE

★ **MY FAIR LADY***
BECKET
DR. STRANGELOVE OR: HOW I LEARNED TO STOP
   WORRYING AND LOVE THE BOMB
MARY POPPINS
ZORBA THE GREEK

ACTOR

★ **REX HARRISON—My Fair Lady**
RICHARD BURTON—Becket
PETER O'TOOLE—Becket
ANTHONY QUINN—Zorba the Greek
PETER SELLERS—Dr. Strangelove...

ACTRESS

★ **JULIE ANDREWS—Mary Poppins***
ANNE BANCROFT—The Pumpkin Eater
SOPHIA LOREN—Marriage Italian Style
DEBBIE REYNOLDS—The Unsinkable Molly Brown
KIM STANLEY—Séance on a Wet Afternoon

SUPPORTING ACTOR

★ **PETER USTINOV—Topkapi**
JOHN GIELGUD—Becket
STANLEY HOLLOWAY—My Fair Lady
EDMOND O'BRIEN—Seven Days in May
LEE TRACY—The Best Man

SUPPORTING ACTRESS

★ **LILA KEDROVA—Zorba the Greek**
GLADYS COOPER—My Fair Lady
EDITH EVANS—The Chalk Garden
GRAYSON HALL—The Night of the Iguana
AGNES MOOREHEAD—Hush...Hush, Sweet Charlotte

DIRECTOR

★ **MY FAIR LADY—George Cukor**
BECKET—Peter Glenville
DR. STRANGELOVE...—Stanley Kubrick
MARY POPPINS—Robert Stevenson
ZORBA THE GREEK—Michael Cacoyannis

CINEMATOGRAPHY (BLACK & WHITE)

★ **ZORBA THE GREEK—Walter Lassally**
THE AMERICANIZATION OF EMILY—Phillip H. Lathrop
FATE IS THE HUNTER—Milton Krasner
HUSH... HUSH, SWEET CHARLOTTE—Joseph Biroc
THE NIGHT OF THE IGUANA—Gabriel Figueroa

CINEMATOGRAPHY (COLOR)

★ **MY FAIR LADY—Harry Stradling**
BECKET—Geoffrey Unsworth
CHEYENNE AUTUMN—William H. Clothier
MARY POPPINS—Edward Colman
THE UNSINKABLE MOLLY BROWN—Daniel L. Fapp

ORIGINAL SCORE

★ **MARY POPPINS—Richard M. & Robert B. Sherman**
BECKET—Laurence Rosenthal
THE FALL OF THE ROMAN EMPIRE—Dimitri Tiomkin
HUSH... HUSH, SWEET CHARLOTTE—Frank De Vol
THE PINK PANTHER—Henry Mancini

MUSICAL ADAPTATION

★ **MY FAIR LADY—André Previn**
A HARD DAY'S NIGHT—George Martin
MARY POPPINS—Irwin Kostal
ROBIN AND THE 7 HOODS—Nelson Riddle
THE UNSINKABLE MOLLY BROWN—Robert Ambruster, Leo
    Amaud, Jack Elliot, Jack Hayes, Calvin Jackson, Leo Shuken

SONG

★ **CHIM CHIM CHER-EE** *from* **Mary Poppins**
DEAR HEART *from* Dear Heart
HUSH... HUSH, SWEET CHARLOTTE *from* Hush... Hush, Sweet
    Charlotte
MY KIND OF TOWN *from* Robin and the 7 Hoods
WHERE LOVE HAS GONE *from* Where Love Has Gone

1966

First Oscars telecast in color.

BEST PICTURE

★ **THE SOUND OF MUSIC**
DARLING
DOCTOR ZHIVAGO
SHIP OF FOOLS
A THOUSAND CLOWNS

ACTOR

★ **LEE MARVIN—Cat Ballou**
RICHARD BURTON—The Spy Who Came in from the Cold
LAURENCE OLIVIER—Othello
ROD STEIGER—The Pawnbroker
OSKAR WERNER—Ship of Fools

ACTRESS

★ **JULIE CHRISTIE—Darling**
JULIE ANDREWS—The Sound of Music
SAMANTHA EGGAR—The Collector
ELIZABETH HARTMAN—A Patch of Blue
SIMONE SIGNORET—Ship of Fools

SUPPORTING ACTOR

★ **MARTIN BALSAM—A Thousand Clowns**
IAN BANNEN—The Flight of the Phoenix
TOM COURTENAY—Doctor Zhivago
MICHAEL DUNN—Ship of Fools
FRANK FINLAY—Othello

SUPPORTING ACTRESS

★ **SHELLEY WINTERS—A Patch of Blue**
RUTH GORDON—Inside Daisy Clover
JOYCE REDMAN—Othello
MAGGIE SMITH—Othello
PEGGY WOOD—The Sound of Music

DIRECTOR

★ **THE SOUND OF MUSIC—Robert Wise**
THE COLLECTOR—William Wyler
DARLING—John Schlesinger
DOCTOR ZHIVAGO—David Lean
THE WOMAN IN THE DUNES—Hiroshi Teshigahara

CINEMATOGRAPHY (BLACK & WHITE)

★ **SHIP OF FOOLS—Ernest Laszlo**
IN HARM'S WAY—Loyal Griggs
KING RAT—Burnett Guffey
MORITURI—Conrad Hall
A PATCH OF BLUE—Robert Burks

CINEMATOGRAPHY (COLOR)

★ **DOCTOR ZHIVAGO—Freddie Young**
THE AGONY AND THE ECSTASY—Leon Shamroy
THE GREAT RACE—Russell Harlan
THE GREATEST STORY EVER TOLD—William C. Mellor and
   Loyal Griggs
THE SOUND OF MUSIC—Ted D. McCord

ORIGINAL SCORE

★ **DOCTOR ZHIVAGO—Maurice Jarre**
THE AGONY AND THE ECSTASY—Alex North
THE GREATEST STORY EVER TOLD—Alfred Newman
A PATCH OF BLUE—Jerry Goldsmith
THE UMBRELLAS OF CHERBOURG—Michel Legrand and
   Jacques Demy

MUSICAL ADAPTATION

★ **THE SOUND OF MUSIC—Irwin Kostal**
CAT BALLOU—Frank De Vol
THE PLEASURE SEEKERS—Lionel Newman & Alexander Courage
A THOUSAND CLOWNS—Don Walker
THE UMBRELLAS OF CHERBOURG—Michel Legrand

SONG

★ **THE SHADOW OF YOUR SMILE** *from* **The Sandpiper**
THE BALLAD OF CAT BALLOU *from* Cat Ballou
I WILL WAIT FOR YOU *from* The Umbrellas of Cherbourg
THE SWEETHEART TREE *from* The Great Race
WHAT'S NEW PUSSYCAT? *from* What's New Pussycat?

1967

Patricia Neal, recovered from stroke, receives standing ovation.
California Governor Ronald Reagan in audience.

BEST PICTURE

★ **A MAN FOR ALL SEASONS**
ALFIE
THE RUSSIANS ARE COMING, THE RUSSIANS ARE COMING
THE SAND PEBBLES
WHO'S AFRAID OF VIRGINIA WOOLF?

ACTOR

★ **PAUL SCOFIELD—A Man for All Seasons**
ALAN ARKIN—The Russians Are Coming, the Russians
 Are Coming
RICHARD BURTON—Who's Afraid of Virginia Woolf?
MICHAEL CAINE—Alfie
STEVE McQUEEN—The Sand Pebbles

ACTRESS

★ **ELIZABETH TAYLOR—Who's Afraid of Virginia Woolf?**
ANOUK AIMÉE—A Man and a Woman
IDA KAMIŃSKA—The Shop on Main Street
LYNN REDGRAVE—Georgy Girl
VANESSA REDGRAVE—Morgan!

SUPPORTING ACTOR

★ **WALTER MATTHAU—The Fortune Cookie**
MAKO—The Sand Pebbles
JAMES MASON—Georgy Girl
GEORGE SEGAL—Who's Afraid of Virginia Woolf?
ROBERT SHAW—A Man for All Seasons

SUPPORTING ACTRESS

★ **SANDY DENNIS—Who's Afraid of Virginia Woolf?**
WENDY HILLER—A Man for All Seasons
JOCELYNE LaGARDE—Hawaii
VIVIEN MERCHANT—Alfie
GERALDINE PAGE—You're a Big Boy Now

DIRECTOR

★ **A MAN FOR ALL SEASONS—Fred Zinnemann**
BLOWUP—Michelangelo Antonioni
A MAN AND A WOMAN—Claude Lelouch
THE PROFESSIONALS—Richard Brooks
WHO'S AFRAID OF VIRGINIA WOOLF?—Mike Nichols

CINEMATOGRAPHY (BLACK & WHITE)

★ **WHO'S AFRAID OF VIRGINIA WOOLF?—Haskell Wexler**
THE FORTUNE COOKIE—Joseph LaShelle
GEORGY GIRL—Kenneth Higgins
IS PARIS BURNING?—Marcel Grignon
SECONDS—James Wong Howe

CINEMATOGRAPHY (COLOR)

★ **A MAN FOR ALL SEASONS—Ted Moore**
FANTASTIC VOYAGE—Ernest Laszlo
HAWAII—Russell Harlan
THE PROFESSIONALS—Conrad Hall
THE SAND PEBBLES—Joseph MacDonald

ORIGINAL SCORE

★ **BORN FREE—John Barry**
THE BIBLE: IN THE BEGINNING—Toshiro Mayuzumi
HAWAII—Elmer Bernstein
THE SAND PEBBLES—Jerry Goldsmith
WHO'S AFRAID OF VIRGINIA WOOLF?—Alex North

MUSICAL ADAPTATION

★ **A FUNNY THING HAPPENED ON THE WAY TO THE FORUM—Ken Thorne**
THE GOSPEL ACCORDING TO ST. MATTHEW—Luis Enriquez Bacalov
RETURN OF THE SEVEN—Elmer Bernstein
THE SINGING NUN—Harry Sukman
STOP THE WORLD - I WANT TO GET OFF—Al Ham

SONG

★ **BORN FREE** *from* **Born Free**
ALFIE *from* Alfie
GEORGY GIRL *from* Georgy Girl
MY WISHING DOLL *from* Hawaii
A TIME FOR LOVE *from* An American Dream

1968

Birth of MPAA film rating system follows long, slow death of Hays Code.

Shortest Speech--Alfred Hitchcock honorary award: "Thank you—very much indeed."

BEST PICTURE

★ **IN THE HEAT OF THE NIGHT**
  BONNIE AND CLYDE
  DOCTOR DOLITTLE
  THE GRADUATE
  GUESS WHO'S COMING TO DINNER

ACTOR

★ **ROD STEIGER—In the Heat of the Night**
  WARREN BEATTY—Bonnie and Clyde
  DUSTIN HOFFMAN—The Graduate
  PAUL NEWMAN—Cool Hand Luke
  SPENCER TRACY—Guess Who's Coming to Dinner

ACTRESS

★ **KATHARINE HEPBURN—Guess Who's Coming
   to Dinner**
  ANNE BANCROFT—The Graduate
  FAYE DUNAWAY—Bonnie and Clyde
  EDITH EVANS—The Whisperers
  AUDREY HEPBURN—Wait Until Dark

SUPPORTING ACTOR

★ **GEORGE KENNEDY—Cool Hand Luke**
  JOHN CASSAVETES—The Dirty Dozen
  GENE HACKMAN—Bonnie and Clyde
  CECIL KELLAWAY—Guess Who's Coming to Dinner
  MICHAEL J. POLLARD—Bonnie and Clyde

SUPPORTING ACTRESS

★ **ESTELLE PARSONS—Bonnie and Clyde**
  CAROL CHANNING—Thoroughly Modern Millie
  MILDRED NATWICK—Barefoot in the Park
  BEAH RICHARDS—Guess Who's Coming to Dinner
  KATHARINE ROSS—The Graduate

DIRECTOR

★ **THE GRADUATE—Mike Nichols**
BONNIE AND CLYDE—Arthur Penn
GUESS WHO'S COMING TO DINNER—Stanley Kramer
IN COLD BLOOD—Richard Brooks
IN THE HEAT OF THE NIGHT—Norman Jewison

CINEMATOGRAPHY

★ **BONNIE AND CLYDE—Burnett Guffey**
CAMELOT—Richard H. Kline
DOCTOR DOLITTLE—Robert Surtees
THE GRADUATE—Robert Surtees
IN COLD BLOOD—Conrad Hall

ART DIRECTION

★ **CAMELOT**
DOCTOR DOLITTLE
GUESS WHO'S COMING TO DINNER
THE TAMING OF THE SHREW
THOROUGHLY MODERN MILLIE

ORIGINAL SCORE

★ **THOROUGHLY MODERN MILLIE—Elmer Bernstein**
COOL HAND LUKE—Lalo Schifrin
DOCTOR DOLITTLE—Leslie Bricusse
FAR FROM THE MADDING CROWD—Richard Rodney
  Bennett
IN COLD BLOOD—Quincy Jones

MUSICAL ADAPTATION

★ **CAMELOT—Alfred Newman and Ken Darby**
DOCTOR DOLITTLE—Lionel Newman & Alexander Courage
GUESS WHO'S COMING TO DINNER—Frank De Vol
THOROUGHLY MODERN MILLIE—André Previn and Joseph
  Gershenson
VALLEY OF THE DOLLS—John Williams

SONG

★ **TALK TO THE ANIMALS** *from* **Doctor Dolittle**
THE BARE NECESSITIES *from* The Jungle Book
THE EYES OF LOVE *from* Banning
THE LOOK OF LOVE *from* Casino Royale
THOROUGHLY MODERN MILLIE *from* Thoroughly Modern
  Millie

1969

Time Magazine decries "vulgar solicitation of votes" that produce wins (particularly Roberton's) based mainly on promotion.

BEST PICTURE

★ **OLIVER!**
  FUNNY GIRL
  THE LION IN WINTER
  RACHEL, RACHEL
  ROMEO AND JULIET

ACTOR

★ **CLIFF ROBERTSON—Charley***
  ALAN ARKIN—The Heart Is a Lonely Hunter
  ALAN BATES—The Fixer
  RON MOODY—Oliver!
  PETER O'TOOLE—The Lion in Winter

ACTRESS

★ **KATHARINE HEPBURN—The Lion in Winter**
★ **BARBRA STREISAND—Funny Girl**   (Tied)
  PATRICIA NEAL—The Subject Was Roses
  VANESSA REDGRAVE—Isadora
  JOANNE WOODWARD—Rachel, Rachel

SUPPORTING ACTOR

★ **JACK ALBERTSON—The Subject Was Roses**
  SEYMOUR CASSEL—Faces
  DANIEL MASSEY—Star!
  JACK WILD—Oliver!
  GENE WILDER—The Producers

SUPPORTING ACTRESS

★ **RUTH GORDON—Rosemary's Baby**
  LYNN CARLIN—Faces
  SONDRA LOCKE—The Heart Is a Lonely Hunter
  KAY MEDFORD—Funny Girl
  ESTELLE PARSONS—Rachel, Rachel

DIRECTOR

★ **OLIVER!—Carol Reed**
2001: A SPACE ODYSSEY—Stanley Kubrick
THE BATTLE OF ALGIERS—Gillo Pontecorvo
THE LION IN WINTER—Anthony Harvey
ROMEO AND JULIET—Franco Zeffirelli

CINEMATOGRAPHY

★ **ROMEO AND JULIET—Pasqualino De Santis**
FUNNY GIRL—Harry Stradling
ICE STATION ZEBRA—Daniel L. Fapp
OLIVER!—Oswald Morris
STAR!—Ernest Laszlo

ART DIRECTION

★ **OLIVER!**
2001: A SPACE ODYSSEY
THE SHOES OF THE FISHERMAN
STAR!
WAR AND PEACE

ORIGINAL SCORE

★ **THE LION IN WINTER—John Barry**
THE FOX—Lalo Schifrin
PLANET OF THE APES—Jerry Goldsmith
THE SHOES OF THE FISHERMAN—Alex North
THE THOMAS CROWN AFFAIR—Michel Legrand

MUSICAL ADAPTATION

★ **OLIVER!—Johnny Green**
FINIAN'S RAINBOW—Ray Heindorf
FUNNY GIRL—Walter Scharf
STAR!—Lennie Hayton
THE YOUNG GIRLS OF ROCHEFORT—Michel Legrand and
Jacques Demy

SONG

★ **THE WINDMILLS OF YOUR MIND** *from* **The Thomas
Crown Affair**
CHITTY CHITTY BANG BANG *from* Chitty Chitty Bang Bang
FOR LOVE OF IVY *from* For Love of Ivy
FUNNY GIRL *from* Funny Girl
STAR! *from* Star!

1970

Only X-rated movie ever to win Best Picture.

BEST PICTURE

★ **MIDNIGHT COWBOY***
  ANNE OF THE THOUSAND DAYS
  BUTCH CASSIDY AND THE SUNDANCE KID
  HELLO, DOLLY!
  Z

ACTOR

★ **JOHN WAYNE—True Grit**
  RICHARD BURTON—Anne of the Thousand Days
  DUSTIN HOFFMAN—Midnight Cowboy
  PETER O'TOOLE—Goodbye, Mr. Chips
  JON VOIGHT—Midnight Cowboy

ACTRESS

★ **MAGGIE SMITH—The Prime of Miss Jean Brodie**
  GENEVIÉVE BUJOLD—Anne of the Thousand Days
  JANE FONDA—They Shoot Horses, Don't They?
  LIZA MINNELLI—The Sterile Cuckoo
  JEAN SIMMONS—The Happy Ending

SUPPORTING ACTOR

★ **GIG YOUNG—They Shoot Horses, Don't They?**
  RUPERT CROSSE—The Reivers
  ELLIOTT GOULD—Bob & Carol & Ted & Alice
  JACK NICHOLSON—Easy Rider
  ANTHONY QUAYLE—Anne of the Thousand Days

SUPPORTING ACTRESS

★ **GOLDIE HAWN—Cactus Flower**
  CATHERINE BURNS—Last Summer
  DYAN CANNON—Bob & Carol & Ted & Alice
  SYLVIA MILES—Midnight Cowboy
  SUSANNAH YORK—They Shoot Horses, Don't They?

DIRECTOR

★ **MIDNIGHT COWBOY—John Schlesinger**
ALICE'S RESTAURANT—Arthur Penn
BUTCH CASSIDY AND THE SUNDANCE KIDD—George Roy Hill
THEY SHOOT HORSES, DON'T THEY?—Sydney Pollack
Z—Costa-Gavras

CINEMATOGRAPHY

★ **BUTCH CASSIDY AND THE SUNDANCE KIDD—Conrad L. Hall**
ANNE OF THE THOUSAND DAYS—Arthur Ibbetson
BOB & CAROL & TED & ALICE—Charles Lang Jr.
HELLO, DOLLY!—Harry Stradling
MAROONED—Daniel L. Fapp

ART DIRECTION

★ **HELLO, DOLLY**
ANNE OF THE THOUSAND DAYS
GAILY, GAILY
SWEET CHARITY
THEY SHOOT HORSES, DON'T THEY?

ORIGINAL SCORE

★ **BUTCH CASSIDY AND THE SUNDANCE KID—Burt Bacharach**
ANNE OF THE THOUSAND DAYS—Georges Delerue
THE REIVERS—John Williams
THE SECRET OF SANTA VITTORIA—Ernest Gold
THE WILD BUNCH—Jerry Fielding

MUSICAL ADAPTATION

★ **HELLO DOLLY!—Lenny Hayton and Lionel Newman**
GOODBYE, MR. CHIPS—Leslie Bricusse and John Williams
PAINT YOUR WAGON—Nelson Riddle
SWEET CHARITY—Cy Coleman
THEY SHOOT HORSES, DON'T THEY?—Johnny Green and Albert Woodbury

SONG

★ **RAINDROPS KEEP FALLIN' ON MY HEAD** *from* **Butch Cassidy and the Sundance Kid**
COME SATURDAY MORNING *from* The Sterile Cuckoo
JEAN *from* The Prime of Miss Jean Brodie
TRUE GRIT *from* True Grit
WHAT ARE YOU DOING THE REST OF YOUR LIFE? *from* The Happy Ending

---

1971

*George C. Scott declines Oscar; calls it a
"two-hour meat parade."*

BEST PICTURE

★ **PATTON**
AIRPORT
FIVE EASY PIECES
LOVE STORY
M*A*S*H

ACTOR

★ **GEORGE C. SCOTT—Patton***
MELVYN DOUGLAS—I Never Sang for My Father
JAMES EARL JONES—The Great White Hope
JACK NICHOLSON—Five Easy Pieces
RYAN O'NEAL—Love Story

ACTRESS

★ **GLENDA JACKSON—Women in Love**
JANE ALEXANDER—The Great White Hope
ALI MacGRAW—Love Story
SARAH MILES—Ryan's Daughter
CARRIE SNODGRESS—Diary of a Mad Housewife

SUPPORTING ACTOR

★ **JOHN MILLS—Ryan's Daughter**
RICHARD S. CASTELLANO—Lovers and Other Strangers
CHIEF DAN GEORGE—Little Big Man
GENE HACKMAN—I Never Sang for My Father
JOHN MARLEY—Love Story

SUPPORTING ACTRESS

★ **HELEN HAYES—Airport**
KAREN BLACK—Five Easy Pieces
LEE GRANT—The Landlord
SALLY KELLERMAN—M*a*s*h
MAUREEN STAPLETON—Airport

DIRECTOR

★ **PATTON—Franklin J. Schaffner**
FELLINI SATYRICON—Federico Fellini
LOVE STORY—Arthur Hiller
M*A*S*H—Robert Altman
WOMEN IN LOVE—Ken Russell

CINEMATOGRAPHY

★ **RYAN'S DAUGHTER—Freddie Young**
AIRPORT—Ernest Laszlo
PATTON—Fred J. Koenekamp
TORA! TORA! TORA!—Osami Furuya, Sinsaku Himeda,
   Masamichi Satoh, Charles F. Wheeler
WOMEN IN LOVE—Billy Williams

ART DIRECTION

★ **PATTON**
AIRPORT
THE MOLLY MAGUIRES
SCROOGE
TORA! TORA! TORA!

DRAMATIC SCORE

★ **LOVE STORY—Francis Lai**
AIRPORT—Alfred Newman
CROMWELL—Frank Cordell
PATTON—Jerry Goldsmith
I GIRASOLI—Henry Mancini

MUSICAL SCORE

★ **LET IT BE—The Beatles**
THE BABY MAKER—Fred Karlin and Tywyth Kymry
A BOY NAMED CHARLIE BROWN—Rod McKuen, John Scott
   Trotter, Bill Meléndez, Al Shean, Vince Guaraldi
DARLING LILI—Henry Mancin and Johnny Mercer
SCROOGE—Leslie Bricusse, Ian Fraser, Herbert W. Spencer

SONG

★ **FOR ALL WE KNOW** *from* **Lovers and Other
   Strangers**
PIECES OF DREAMS *from* Pieces of Dreams
THANK YOU VERY MUCH *from* Scrooge
TILL LOVE TOUCHES YOUR LIFE *from* Madron
WHISTLING AWAY THE DARK *from* Darling Lili

Dorothy Chandler Pavilion, Los Angeles   April 15, 1971

1972

*Charlie Chaplin gets honorary award
and 12-minute standing ovation.*

BEST PICTURE

★ **THE FRENCH CONNECTION**
A CLOCKWORK ORANGE
FIDDLER ON THE ROOF
THE LAST PICTURE SHOW
NICHOLAS AND ALEXANDRA

ACTOR

★ **GENE HACKMAN—The French Connection**
PETER FINCH—Sunday Bloody Sunday
WALTER MATTHAU—Kotch
GEORGE C. SCOTT—The Hospital
TOPOL—Fiddler on the Roof

ACTRESS

★ **JANE FONDA—Klute**
JULIE CHRISTIE—McCabe & Mrs. Miller
GLENDA JACKSON—Sunday Bloody Sunday
VANESSA REDGRAVE—Mary, Queen of Scots
JANET SUZMAN—Nicholas and Alexandra

SUPPORTING ACTOR

★ **BEN JOHNSON—The Last Picture Show**
JEFF BRIDGES—The Last Picture Show
LEONARD FREY—Fiddler on the Roof
RICHARD JAECKEL—Sometimes a Great Notion
ROY SCHEIDER—The French Connection

SUPPORTING ACTRESS

★ **CLORIS LEACHMAN—The Last Picture Show**
ANN-MARGRET—Carnal Knowledge
ELLEN BURSTYN—The Last Picture Show
BARBARA HARRIS—Who Is Harry Kellerman and Why
    Is He Saying Those Terrible Things About Me?
MARGARET LEIGHTON—The Go-Between

DIRECTOR

★ **THE FRENCH CONNECTION—William Friedkin**
A CLOCKWORK ORANGE—Stanley Kubrick
FIDDLER ON THE ROOF—Norman Jewison
THE LAST PICTURE SHOW—Peter Bogdanovich
SUNDAY BLOODY SUNDAY—John Schlesinger

CINEMATOGRAPHY

★ **FIDDLER ON THE ROOF—Oswald Morris**
THE FRENCH CONNECTION—Owen Roizman
THE LAST PICTURE SHOW—Robert L. Surtees
NICHOLAS AND ALEXANDRA—Freddie Young
SUMMER OF '42—Robert L. Surtees

ART DIRECTION

★ **NICHOLAS AND ALEXANDRA**
THE ANDROMEDA STRAIN
BEDKNOBS AND BROOMSTICKS
FIDDLER ON THE ROOF
MARY, QUEEN OF SCOTS

DRAMATIC SCORE

★ **SUMMER OF '42—Michel Legrand**
MARY, QUEEN OF SCOTS—John Barry
NICHOLAS AND ALEXANDRA—Richard Rodney Bennett
SHAFT—Isaac Hayes
STRAW DOGS—Jerry Fielding

MUSICAL ADAPTATION

★ **FIDDLER ON THE ROOF—John Williams**
BEDKNOBS AND BROOMSTICKS—Irwin Kostal, Richard M.
and Robert B. Sherman
THE BOY FRIEND—Peter Maxwell Davies and Peter
Greenwell
TCHAIKOVSKY—Dimitri Tiomkin
WILLY WONKA & THE CHOCOLATE FACTORY—Walter
Scharf, Leslie Bricusse, Anthony Newley

SONG

★ **THEME FROM SHAFT** *from* **Shaft**
THE AGE OF NOT BELIEVING *from* Bedknobs and
Broomsticks
ALL HIS CHILDREN *from* Sometimes a Great Notion
BLESS THE BEASTS AND CHILDREN *from* Bless the
Beasts and Children
LIFE IS WHAT YOU MAKE IT *from* Kotch

1973

BEST PICTURE

★ **THE GODFATHER**
CABARET
DELIVERANCE
THE EMIGRANTS
SOUNDER

ACTOR

★ **MARLON BRANDO—The Godfather***
MICHAEL CAINE—Sleuth
LAURENCE OLIVIER—Sleuth
PETER O'TOOLE—The Ruling Class
PAUL WINFIELD—Sounder

ACTRESS

★ **LIZA MINNELLI—Cabaret**
DIANA ROSS—Lady Sings the Blues
MAGGIE SMITH—Travels with My Aunt
CICELY TYSON—Sounder
LIV ULLMANN—The Emigrants

SUPPORTING ACTOR

★ **JOEL GREY—Cabaret**
EDDIE ALBERT—The Heartbreak Kid
JAMES CAAN—The Godfather
ROBERT DUVALL—The Godfather
AL PACINO—The Godfather

SUPPORTING ACTRESS

★ **EILEEN HECKART—Butterflies Are Free**
JEANNIE BERLIN—The Heartbreak Kid
GERALDINE PAGE—Pete 'n' Tillie
SUSAN TYRRELL—Fat City
SHELLEY WINTERS—The Poseidon Adventure

DIRECTOR

★ **CABARET—Bob Fosse**
DELIVERANCE—John Boorman
THE EMIGRANTS—Jan Troell
THE GODFATHER—Francis Ford Coppola
SLEUTH—Joseph L. Mankiewicz

CINEMATOGRAPHY

★ **CABARET—Geoffrey Unsworth**
1776—Harry Stradling Jr.
BUTTERFLIES ARE FREE—Charles Lang Jr.
THE POSEIDON ADVENTURE—Harold E. Stine
TRAVELS WITH MY AUNT—Douglas Slocombe

ART DIRECTION

★ **CABARET**
LADY SINGS THE BLUES
THE POSEIDON ADVENTURE
TRAVELS WITH MY AUNT
YOUNG WINSTON

DRAMATIC SCORE

★ **LIMELIGHT—Charlie Chaplin, Raymond Rasch, Larry Russell**
IMAGES—John Williams
NAPOLEON AND Samantha—Buddy Baker
THE POSEIDON ADVENTURE—John Williams
SLEUTH—John Addison

MUSICAL ADAPTATION

★ **CABARET—Ralph Burns**
LADY SINGS THE BLUES—Gil Askey
MAN OF LA MANCHA—Laurence Rosenthal

SONG

★ **THE MORNING AFTER** *from* **The Poseidon Adventure**
BEN *from* Ben
COME FOLLOW, FOLLOW ME *from* The Little Ark
MARMALADE, MOLASSES & HONEY *from* The Life and Times of Judge Roy Bean
STRANGE ARE THE WAYS OF LOVE *from* The Stepmother

1974

Streaker interrupts unflappable presenter David Niven, who bemoans the man's only claim to fame: "showing his shortcomings."

BEST PICTURE

★ **THE STING**
AMERICAN GRAFFITI
CRIES AND WHISPERS
THE EXORCIST
A TOUCH OF CLASS

ACTOR

★ **JACK LEMMON—Save the Tiger**
MARLON BRANDO—Last Tango in Paris
JACK NICHOLSON—The Last Detail
AL PACINO—Serpico
ROBERT REDFORD—The Sting

ACTRESS

★ **GLENDA JACKSON—A Touch of Class**
ELLEN BURSTYN—The Exorcist
MARSHA MASON—Cinderella Liberty
BARBRA STREISAND—The Way We Were
JOANNE WOODWARD—Summer Wishes, Winter Dreams

SUPPORTING ACTOR

★ **JOHN HOUSEMAN—The Paper Chase**
VINCENT GARDENIA—Bang the Drum Slowly
JACK GILFORD—Save the Tiger
JASON MILLER—The Exorcist
RANDY QUAID—The Last Detail

SUPPORTING ACTRESS

★ **TATUM O'NEAL—Paper Moon**
LINDA BLAIR—The Exorcist
CANDY CLARK—American Graffiti
MADELINE KAHN—Paper Moon
SYLVIA SIDNEY—Summer Wishes, Winter Dreams

DIRECTOR

★ **THE STING—George Roy Hill**
AMERICAN GRAFFITI—George Lucas
CRIES AND WHISPERS—ingmar Bergman
THE EXORCIST—William Friedkin
LAST TANGO IN PARIS—Bernardo Bertolucci

CINEMATOGRAPHY

★ **CRIES AND WHISPERS—Sven Nykvist**
THE EXORSIST—Owen Roizman
JOHATHAN LIVINGSTON SEAGULL—Jack Couffer
THE STING—Robert Surtees
THE WAY WE WERE—Harry Stradling Jr.

ART DIRECTION

★ **THE STING**
BROTHER SUN, SISTER MOON
THE EXORCIST
TOM SAWYER
THE WAY WE WERE

DRAMATIC SCORE

★ **THE WAY WE WERE—Marvin Hamlisch**
CINDERELLA LIBERTY—John Williams
THE DAY OF THE DOLPHIN—Georges Delerue
PAPILLON—Jerry Goldsmith
A TOUCH OF CLASS—John Cameron

MUSICAL ADAPTATION

★ **THE STING—Marvin Hamlisch**
JESUS CHRIST SUPERSTAR—André Previn, Herbert W.
   Spencer, Andrew Lloyd Weber
TOM SAWYER—Richard M. and Robert B. Sherman,
   John Williams

SONG

★ **THE WAY WE WERE** *from* **The Way We Were**
ALL THAT LOVE WENT TO WASTE *from* A Touch of Class
LIVE AND LET DIE *from* Live and Let Die
LOVE *from* Robin Hood
(You're So) NICE TO BE AROUND *from* Cinderella Liberty

1975

Charlie Chaplin knighted by Queen Elizabeth II.

BEST PICTURE

★ **THE GODFATHER: PART II**
CHINATOWN
THE CONVERSATION
LENNY
THE TOWERING INFERNO

ACTOR

★ **ART CARNEY—Harry and Tonto**
ALBERT FINNEY—Murder on the Orient Express
DUSTIN HOFFMAN—Lenny
JACK NICHOLSON—Chinatown
AL PACINO—The Godfather: Part II

ACTRESS

★ **ELLEN BURSTYN—Alice Doesn't Live Here Anymore**
DIAHANN CARROLL—Claudine
FAYE DUNAWAY—Chinatown
VALERIE PERRINE—Lenny
GENA ROWLANDS—A Woman Under the Influence

SUPPORTING ACTOR

★ **ROBERT DE NIRO—The Godfather: Part II**
FRED ASTAIRE—The Towering Inferno
JEFF BRIDGES—Thunderbolt and Lightfoot
MICHAEL V. GAZZO—The Godfather: Part II
LEE STRASBERG—The Godfather: Part II

SUPPORTING ACTRESS

★ **INGRID BERGMAN—Murder on the Orient Express**
VALENTINA CORTESE—Day for Night
MADELINE KAHN—Blazing Saddles
DIANE LADD—Alice Doesn't Live Here Anymore
TALIA SHIRE—The Godfather: Part II

DIRECTOR

★ **THE GODFATHER: PART II—Francis Ford Coppola**
CHINATOWN—Roman Polanski
DAY FOR NIGHT—François Truffaut
LENNY—Bob Fosse
A WOMAN UNDER THE INFLUENCE—John Cassavetes

CINEMATOGRAPHY

★ **THE TOWERING INFERNO—Joseph Biroc and Fred J. Koenekamp**
CHINATOWN—John A. Alonzo
EARTHQUAKE—Philip Lathrop
LENNY—Bruce Surtees
MURDER ON THE ORIENT EXPRESS—Geoffrey Unsworth

ART DIRECTION

★ **THE GODFATHER: PART II**
CHINATOWN
EARTHQUAKE
THE ISLAND AT THE TOP OF THE WORLD
THE TOWERING INFERNO

DRAMATIC SCORE

★ **THE GODFATHER: PART II—Nino Rota and Carmine Coppola**
CHINATOWN—Jerry Goldsmith
MURDER ON THE ORIENT EXPRESS—Richard Rodney Bennett
SHANKS—Alex North
THE TOWERING INFERNO—John Williams

MUSICAL ADAPTATION

★ **THE GREAT GATSBY—Nelson Riddle**
THE LITTLE PRINCE—Alan Jay Lerner, Frederick Loewe, Angela Morley, Douglas Gamley
PHANTOM OF THE PARADISE—Paul Williams and George Aliceson Tipton

SONG

★ **WE MAY NEVER LOVE LIKE THIS AGAIN** *from* **The Towering Inferno**
BENJI'S THEME (I Feel Love) *from* Benji
BLAZING SADDLES *from* Blazing Saddles
LITTLE PRINCE *from* The Little Prince
WHEREVER LOVE TAKES ME *from* Gold

1976

BEST PICTURE

★ **ONE FLEW OVER THE CUCKOO'S NEST**
BARRY LYNDON
DOG DAY AFTERNOON
JAWS
NASHVILLE

ACTOR

★ **JACK NICHOLSON—One Flew Over the Cuckoo's Nest**
WALTER MATTHAU—The Sunshine Boys
AL PACINO—Dog Day Afternoon
MAXIMILIAN SCHELL—The Man in the Glass Booth
JAMES WHITMORE—Give 'em Hell, Harry!

ACTRESS

★ **LOUISE FLETCHER—One Flew Over the Cuckoo's Nest**
ISABELLE ADJANI—The Story of Adele H.
ANN-MARGRET—Tommy
GLENDA JACKSON—Hedda
CAROL KANE—Hester Street

SUPPORTING ACTOR

★ **GEORGE BURNS—The Sunshine Boys***
BRAD DOURIF—One Flew Over the Cuckoo's Nest
BURGESS MEREDITH—The Day of the Locust
CHRIS SARANDON—Dog Day Afternoon
JACK WARDEN—Shampoo

SUPPORTING ACTRESS

★ **LEE GRANT—Shampoo**
RONEE BLAKLEY—Nashville
SYLVIA MILES—Farewell, My Lovely
LILY TOMLIN—Nashville
BRENDA VACCARO—Once Is Not Enough

DIRECTOR

★ **ONE FLEW OVER THE CUCKOO'S NEST—Miloš Forman**
AMARCORD—Federico Fellini
BARRY LYNDON—Stanley Kubrick
DOG DAY AFTERNOON—Sidney Lumet
NASHVILLE—Robert Altman

CINEMATOGRAPHY

★ **BARRY LYNDON—John Alcott**
THE DAY OF THE LOCUST—Conrad Hall
FUNNY LADY—James Wong Howe
THE HINDENBURG—Robert Surtees
ONE FLEW OVER THE CUCKOO'S NEST—Bill Butler and Haskell Wexlet

ART DIRECTION

★ **BARRY LYNDON**
THE HINDENBURG
THE MAN WHO WOULD BE KING
SHAMPOO
THE SUNSHINE BOYS

DRAMATIC SCORE

★ **JAWS—John Williams**
BIRDS DO IT, BEES DO IT—Gerald Fried
BITE THE BULLET—Alex North
ONE FLEW OVER THE CUCKOO'S NEST—Jack Nitzsche
THE WIND AND THE LION—Jerry Goldsmith

MUSICAL ADAPTATION

★ **BARRY LYNDON—Leonard Rosenman**
FUNNY LADY—Peter Matz
TOMMY—Pete Townshend

SONG

★ **I'M EASY** *from* **Nashville**
DO YOU KNOW WHERE YOU'RE GOING TO *from* Mahogany
HOW LUCKY CAN YOU GET *from* Funny Lady
NOW THAT WE'RE IN LOVE *from* Whiffs
RICHARD'S WINDOW *from* The Other Side of the Mountain

1977

Peter Finch Posthumous win.

BEST PICTURE

★ **ROCKY**
ALL THE PRESIDENT'S MEN
BOUND FOR GLORY
NETWORK
TAXI DRIVER

ACTOR

★ **PETER FINCH—Network***
ROBERT DE NIRO—Taxi Driver
GIANCARLO GIANNINI—Seven Beauties
WILLIAM HOLDEN—Network
SYLVESTER STALLONE—Rocky

ACTRESS

★ **FAYE DUNAWAY—Network**
MARIE-CHRISTINE BARRAULT—Cousin Cousine
TALIA SHIRE—Rocky
SISSY SPACEK—Carrie
LIV ULLMANN—Face to Face

SUPPORTING ACTOR

★ **JASON ROBARDS—All the President's Men**
NED BEATTY—Network
BURGESS MEREDITH—Rocky
LAURENCE OLIVIER—Marathon Man
BURT YOUNG—Rocky

SUPPORTING ACTRESS

★ **BEATRICE STRAIGHT—Network**
JANE ALEXANDER—All the President's Men
JODIE FOSTER—Taxi Driver
LEE GRANT—Voyage of the Damned
PIPER LAURIE—Carrie

DIRECTOR

★ **ROCKY—John G. Avildsen**
ALL THE PRESIDENT'S MEN—Alan J. Pakula
FACE TO FACE—Ingmar Bergman
NETWORK—Sidney Lumet
SEVEN BEAUTIES—Lina Wertmüller

CINEMATOGRAPHY

★ **BOUND FOR GLORY—Haskell Wexler**
KING KONG—Richard H. Kline
LOGAN'S RUN—Ernest Laszlo
NETWORK—Owen Roizman
A STAR IS BORN—Robert L. Surtees

ART DIRECTION

★ **ALL THE PRESIDENT'S MEN**
THE INCREDIBLE SARAH
THE LAST TYCOON
LOGAN'S RUN
THE SHOOTIST

DRAMATIC SCORE

★ **THE OMEN—Jerry Goldsmith**
OBSESSION—Bernard Hermann
THE OUTLAW JOSEY WALES—Jerry Feilding
TAXI DRIVER—Bernard Hermann
VOYAGE OF THE DAMNED—Lalo Schifrin

MUSICAL ADAPTATION

★ **BOUND FOR GLORY—Leonard Rosenman**
BUGSY MALONE—Paul Williams
A STAR IS BORN—Roger Kellaway

SONG

★ **EVERGREEN** *from* **A Star Is Born**
AVE SATANI *from* The Omen
COME TO ME *from* The Pink Panther Strikes Again
GONNA FLY NOW *from* Rocky
A WORLD THAT NEVER WAS *from* Half a House

1978

Politically charged speech by Redgrave draws hisses and boos and chastisement from Paddy Chayefsky during his presentation (to loud applause).

BEST PICTURE

★ **ANNIE HALL**
   THE GOODBYE GIRL
   JULIA
   STAR WARS
   THE TURNING POINT

ACTOR

★ **RICHARD DREYFUSS—The Goodbye Girl**
   WOODY ALLEN—Annie Hall
   RICHARD BURTON—Equus
   MARCELLO MASTROIANNI—A Special Day
   JOHN TRAVOLTA—Saturday Night Fever

ACTRESS

★ **DIANE KEATON—Annie Hall**
   ANNE BANCROFT—The Turning Point
   JANE FONDA—Julia
   SHIRLEY MacLAINE—The Turning Point
   MARSHA MASON—The Goodbye Girl

SUPPORTING ACTOR

★ **JASON ROBARDS—Julia**
   MIKHAIL BARYSHNIKOV—The Turning Point
   PETER FIRTH—Equus
   ALEC GUINNESS—Star Wars
   MAXIMILIAN SCHELL—Julia

SUPPORTING ACTRESS

★ **VANESSA REDGRAVE—Julia***
   LESLIE BROWNE—The Turning Point
   QUINN CUMMINGS—The Goodbye Girl
   MELINDA DILLON—Close Encounters of the Third Kind
   TUESDAY WELD—Looking for Mr. Goodbar

DIRECTOR

★ **ANNIE HALL—Woody Allen**
  CLOSE ENCOUNTERS OF THE THIRD KIND—Steven
    Spielberg
  JULIA—Fred Zinnemann
  STAR WARS—George Lucas
  THE TURNING POINT—Herbert Ross

CINEMATOGRAPHY

★ **CLOSE ENCOUNTERS OF THE THIRD KIND—Vilmos
  Zsigmond**
  ISLANDS IN THE STREAM—Fred J. Koenekamp
  JULIA—Douglas Slocombe
  LOOKING FOR MR. GOODBAR—William A. Fraker
  THE TURNING POINT—Robert Surtees

VISUAL EFFECTS

★ **STAR WARS**
  CLOSE ENCOUNTERS OF THE THIRD KIND

DRAMATIC SCORE

★ **STAR WARS—John Williams**
  JULIA—Georges Delerue
  THE SPY WHO LOVED ME—Marvin Hamlisch
  MOHAMMAD, MESSENGER OF GOD—Maurice Jarre
  CLOSE ENCOUNTERS OF THE THIRD KIND—John Williams

MUSICAL ADAPTATION

★ **A LITTLE NIGHT MUSIC—Jonathan Tunick**
  PETE'S DRAGON—Al Kasha, Joel Hirschhorn, Irwin Kostal
  THE SLIPPER AND THE ROSE—Richard M. and Robert B.
    Sherman, Angela Morley

SONG

★ **YOU LIGHT UP MY LIFE** *from* **You Light Up My Life**
  CANDLE ON THE WATER *from* Pete's Dragon
  NOBODY DOES IT BETTER *from* The Spy Who Loved Me
  SOMEONE'S WAITING FOR YOU *from* The Rescuers
  THE SLIPPER AND THE ROSE WALTZ *from* The Slipper
    and the Rose

Dorothy Chandler Pavilion, Los Angeles   April 3, 1978

1979

Demonstrators against DEER HUNTER *call it racist and false portrayal of Vietnam War; 13 arrests made.*

BEST PICTURE

★ **THE DEER HUNTER**
COMING HOME
HEAVEN CAN WAIT
MIDNIGHT EXPRESS
AN UNMARRIED WOMAN

ACTOR

★ **JON VOIGHT—Coming Home**
WARREN BEATTY—Heaven Can Wait
GARY BUSEY—The Buddy Holly Story
ROBERT DE NIRO—The Deer Hunter
LAURENCE OLIVIER—The Boys from Brazil

ACTRESS

★ **JANE FONDA—Coming Home**
INGRID BERGMAN—Autumn Sonata
ELLEN BURSTYN—Same Time, Next Year
JILL CLAYBURGH—An Unmarried Woman
GERALDINE PAGE—Interiors

SUPPORTING ACTOR

★ **CHRISTOPHER WALKEN—The Deer Hunter**
BRUCE DERN—Coming Home
RICHARD FARNSWORTH—Comes a Horseman
JOHN HURT—Midnight Express
JACK WARDEN—Heaven Can Wait

SUPPORTING ACTRESS

★ **MAGGIE SMITH—California Suite**
DYAN CANNON—Heaven Can Wait
PENELOPE MILFORD—Coming Home
MAUREEN STAPLETON—Interiors
MERYL STREEP—The Deer Hunter

DIRECTOR

★ **THE DEER HUNTER—Michael Cimino**
COMING HOME—Hal Ashby
HEAVEN CAN WAIT—Warren Beatty and Buck Henry
INTERIORS—Woody Allen
MIDNIGHT EXPRESS—Alan Parker

CINEMATOGRAPHY

★ **DAYS OF HEAVEN—Néstor Almendros**
THE DEER HUNTER—Vilmos Zsigmond
HEAVEN CAN WAIT—William A. Fraker
SAME TIME, NEXT YEAR—Robert Surtees
THE WIZ—Oswald Morris

VISUAL EFFECTS

★ **SUPERMAN**

ART DIRECTION

★ **HEAVEN CAN WAIT**
THE BRINK'S JOB
CALIFORNIA SUITE
INTERIORS
THE WIZ

DRAMATIC SCORE

★ **MIDNIGHT EXPRESS—Giorgio Moroder**
THE BOYS FROM BRAZIL—Jerry Goldsmith
DAYS OF HEAVEN—Ennio Morricone
HEAVEN CAN WAIT—Dave Grusin
SUPERMAN—John Williams

MUSICAL SCORE

★ **THE BUDDY HOLLY STORY—Joe Renzetti**
PRETTY BABY—Jerry Wexler
THE WIZ—Quincy Jones

SONG

★ **LAST DANCE** *from* **Thank God It's Friday**
   Paul Jabara
HOPELESSLY DEVOTED TO YOU *from* Grease
THE LAST TIME I FELT LIKE THIS *from* Same Time, Next Year
READY TO TAKE A CHANCE AGAIN *from* Foul Play
WHEN YOU'RE LOVED *from* The Magic of Lassie

1980

Youngest (8-yrs-old) ever to compete for acting Oscar.

BEST PICTURE

★ **KRAMER vs. KRAMER**
ALL THAT JAZZ
APOCALYPSE NOW
BREAKING AWAY
NORMA RAE

ACTOR

★ **DUSTIN HOFFMAN—Kramer vs. Kramer**
JACK LEMMON—The China Syndrome
AL PACINO—...And Justice for All
ROY SCHEIDER—All That Jazz
PETER SELLERS—Being There

ACTRESS

★ **SALLY FIELD—Norma Rae**
JILL CLAYBURGH—Starting Over
JANE FONDA—The China Syndrome
MARSHA MASON—Chapter Two
BETTE MIDLER—The Rose

SUPPORTING ACTOR

★ **MELVYN DOUGLAS—Being There**
ROBERT DUVALL—Apocalypse Now
FREDERIC FORREST—The Rose
JUSTIN HENRY—Kramer vs. Kramer*
MICKEY ROONEY—The Black Stallion

SUPPORTING ACTRESS

★ **MERYL STREEP—Kramer vs. Kramer**
JANE ALEXANDER—Kramer vs. Kramer
BARBARA BARRIE—Breaking Away
CANDICE BERGEN—Starting Over
MARIEL HEMINGWAY—Manhattan

DIRECTOR

★ **KRAMER vs. KRAMER—Robert Benton**
ALL THAT JAZZ—Bob Fosse
APOCALYPSE NOW—Francis Ford Coppola
BREAKING AWAY—Peter Yates
LA CAGE AUX FOLLES—Édouard Molinaro

CINEMATOGRAPHY

★ **APOCALYPSE NOW—Vittorio Storaro**
1941—William A. Fraker
ALL THAT JAZZ—Giuseppe Rotunno
THE BLACK HOLE—Frank Phillips
KRAMER vs. KRAMER—Nestor Almendros

VISUAL EFFECTS

★ **ALIEN**   1941
THE BLACK HOLE   MOONRAKER
STAR TREK: THE MOTION PICTURE

ART DIRECTION

★ **ALL THAT JAZZ**   ALIEN
APOCALYPSE NOW   THE CHINA SYNDROME
STAR TREK: THE MOTION PICTURE

DRAMATIC SCORE

★ **A LITTLE ROMANCE—Georges Delerue**
10—Henry Mancini
THE AMITYVILLE HORROR—Lalo Schifrin
THE CHAMP—Dave Grusin
STAR TREK: THE MOTION PICTURE—Jerry Goldsmith

MUSICAL SCORE

★ **ALL THAT JAZZ—Ralph Burns**
BREAKING AWAY—Patrick Williams
THE MUPPET MOVIE—Paul Williams and Kenny Ascher

SONG

★ **IT GOES LIKE IT GOES** *from* **Norma Rae**
I'LL NEVER SAY GOODBYE *from* The Promise
IT'S EASY TO SAY *from* 10
RAINBOW CONNECTION *from* The Muppet Movie
THROUGH THE EYES OF LOVE *from* Ice Castles

Dorothy Chandler Pavilion, Los Angeles   April 14, 1980

1981

*Ceremony postponed due to March 30
assassination attempt on President Reagan.*

BEST PICTURE

★ **ORDINARY PEOPLE**
COAL MINER'S DAUGHTER
THE ELEPHANT MAN
RAGING BULL
TESS

ACTOR

★ **ROBERT DE NIRO—Raging Bull**
ROBERT DUVALL—The Great Santini
JOHN HURT—The Elephant Man
JACK LEMMON—Tribute
PETER O'TOOLE—The Stunt Man

ACTRESS

★ **SISSY SPACEK—Coal Miner's Daughter**
ELLEN BURSTYN—Resurrection
GOLDIE HAWN—Private Benjamin
MARY TYLER MOORE—Ordinary People
GENA ROWLANDS—Gloria

SUPPORTING ACTOR

★ **TIMOTHY HUTTON—Ordinary People**
JUDD HIRSCH—Ordinary People
MICHAEL O'KEEFE—The Great Santini
JOE PESCI—Raging Bull
JASON ROBARDS—Melvin and Howard

SUPPORTING ACTRESS

★ **MARY STEENBURGEN—Melvin and Howard**
EILEEN BRENNAN—Private Benjamin
EVA LE GALLIENNE—Resurrection
CATHY MORIARTY—Raging Bull
DIANA SCARWID—Inside Moves

DIRECTOR

★ **ORDINARY PEOPLE—Robert Redford**
   THE ELEPHANT MAN—David Lynch
   RAGING BULL—Martin Scorsese
   THE STUNT MAN—Richard Rush
   TESS—Roman Polanski

CINEMATOGRAPHY

★ **TESS—Geoffrey Unswort and Ghislain Cloquet**
   THE BLUE LAGOON—Néstor Almendros
   COAL MINER'S DAUGHTER—Raif D. Bode
   THE FORMULA—James Crabe
   RAGING BULL—Michael Chapman

VISUAL EFFECTS

★ **THE EMPIRE STRIKES BACK**

ART DIRECTION

★ **TESS**
   COAL MINER'S DAUGHTER
   THE ELEPHANT MAN
   THE EMPIRE STRIKES BACK
   KAGEMUSHA

SCORE

★ **FAME—Michael Gore**
   ALTERED STATES—John Corigliano
   THE ELEPHANT MAN—John Morris
   THE EMPIRE STRIKES BACK—John Williams
   TESS—Philippe Sarde

SONG

★ **FAME** *from* **Fam**e
   9 TO 5 *from* 9 to 5
   ON THE ROAD AGAIN *from* Honeysuckle Rose
   OUT HERE ON MY OWN *from* Fame
   PEOPLE ALONE *from* The Competition

1982

*To end rating wars, future NCAA basketball
games will be Monday following Oscar night.*

BEST PICTURE

★ **CHARIOTS OF FIRE**
ATLANTIC CITY
ON GOLDEN POND
RAIDERS OF THE LOST ARK
REDS

ACTOR

★ **HENRY FONDA—On Golden Pond**
WARREN BEATTY—Reds
BURT LANCASTER—Atlantic City
DUDLEY MOORE—Arthur
PAUL NEWMAN—Absence of Malice

ACTRESS

★ **KATHARINE HEPBURN—On Golden Pond**
DIANE KEATON—Reds
MARSHA MASON—Only When I Laugh
SUSAN SARANDON—Atlantic City
MERYL STREEP—The French Lieutenant's Woman

SUPPORTING ACTOR

★ **JOHN GIELGUD—Arthur**
JAMES COCO—Only When I Laugh
IAN HOLM—Chariots of Fire
JACK NICHOLSON—Reds
HOWARD E. ROLLINS JR.—Ragtime

SUPPORTING ACTRESS

★ **MAUREEN STAPLETON—Reds**
MELINDA DILLON—Absence of Malice
JANE FONDA—On Golden Pond
JOAN HACKETT—Only When I Laugh
ELIZABETH McGOVERN—Ragtime

DIRECTOR

★ **REDS—Warren Beatty**
ATLANTIC CITY—Louis Malle
CHARIOTS OF FIRE—Hugh Hudson
ON GOLDEN POND—Mark Rydell
RAIDERS OF THE LOST ARK—Steven Spielberg

CINEMATOGRAPHY

★ **REDS—Vittorio Storaro**
EXCALIBUR—Alex Thomson
ON GOLDEN POND—Billy Williams
RAGTIME—Miroslav Ondříček
RAIDERS OF THE LOST ARK—Douglas Slocombe

VISUAL EFFECTS

★ **RAIDERS OF THE LOST ARC**
DRAGONSLAYER

ART DIRECTION

★ **RAIDERS OF THE LOST ARC**
THE FRENCH LIEUTENANT'S WOMAN
HEAVEN'S GATE
RAGTIME
REDS

SCORE

★ **CHARIOTS OF FIRE—Vangelis**
DRAGONSLAYER—Alex North
ON GOLDEN POND—Dave Grusin
RAGTIME—Randy Newman
RAIDERS OF THE LOST ARK—John Williams

SONG

★ **ARTHUR'S THEME (Best That You Can Do)** *from* **Arthur**
ENDLESS LOVE *from* Endless Love
THE FIRST TIME IT HAPPENS *from* The Great Muppet Caper
FOR YOUR EYES ONLY *from* For Your Eyes Only
ONE MORE HOUR *from* Ragtime

1983

Presenter veteran Oscars host Bob Hope and honorary recipient Mickey Rooney vie for longest standing ovation.

BEST PICTURE

★ **GANDHI**
E.T. THE EXTRA-TERRESTRIAL
MISSING
TOOTSIE
THE VERDICT

ACTOR

★ **BEN KINGSLEY—Gandhi**
DUSTIN HOFFMAN—Tootsie
JACK LEMMON—Missing
PAUL NEWMAN—The Verdict
PETER O'TOOLE—My Favorite Year

ACTRESS

★ **MERYL STREEP—Sophie's Choice**
JULIE ANDREWS—Victor/Victoria
JESSICA LANGE—Frances
SISSY SPACEK—Missing
DEBRA WINGER—An Officer and a Gentleman

SUPPORTING ACTOR

★ **LOUIS GOSSETT JR.—An Officer and a Gentleman**
CHARLES DURNING—The Best Little Whorehouse in Texas
JOHN LITHGOW—The World According to Garp
JAMES MASON—The Verdict
ROBERT PRESTON—Victor/Victoria

SUPPORTING ACTRESS

★ **JESSICA LANGE—Tootsie**
GLENN CLOSE—The World According to Garp
TERI GARR—Tootsie
KIM STANLEY—Frances
LESLEY ANN WARREN—Victor/Victoria

DIRECTOR

★ **GANDHI—Richard Attenborough**
DAS BOOT—Wolfgang Peterson
E.T. the Extra-Terrestrial—Steven Speilberg
TOOTSIE—Sydney Pollack
THE VERDICT—Sidney Lumet

CINEMATOGRAPHY

★ **GANDHI—Billy Williams and Ronnie Taylor**
DAS BOOT—Jost Vacano
E.T. the Extra-Terrestrial—Allen Daviau
SOPHIE'S CHOICE—Néstor Almendros
TOOTSIE—Owen Roizman

VISUAL EFFECTS

★ **E.T. THE EXTRA-TERRESTRIAL**
BLADE RUNNER
POLTERGEIST

ART DIRECTION

★ **GANDHI**
ANNIE
BLADE RUNNER
LA TRAVIATA
VICTOR/VICTORIA

DRAMATIC SCORE

★ **E.T. THE EXTRA-TERRESTRIAL—John Williams**
GANDHI—Ravi Shankar and George Fenton
AN OFFICER AND A GENTLEMAN—Jack Nitzsche
POLTERGEIST—Jerry Goldsmith
SOPHIE'S CHOICE—Marvin Hamlisch

MUSICAL SCORE

★ **VICTOR/VICTORIA—Henry Mancini & Leslie Bricusse**
ANNIE—Ralph Burns
ONE FROM THE HEART—Tom Waits

SONG

★ **UP WHERE WE BELONG** *from* **An Officer and a Gentleman**
EYE OF THE TIGER *from* Rocky III
HOW DO YOU KEEP THE MUSIC PLAYING *from* Best Friends
IF WE WERE IN LOVE *from* YES, GEORGIO
IT MIGHT BE YOU *from* Tootsie

1984

New computer clock warns awardees how much speech time they have.
(Music ready if they ignore it.)

BEST PICTURE

★ **TERMS OF ENDEARMENT**
   THE BIG CHILL
   THE DRESSER
   THE RIGHT STUFF
   TENDER MERCIES

ACTOR

★ **ROBERT DUVALL—Tender Mercies**
   MICHAEL CAINE—Educating Rita
   TOM CONTI—Reuben, Reuben
   TOM COURTENAY—The Dresser
   ALBERT FINNEY—The Dresser

ACTRESS

★ **SHIRLEY MacLAINE—Terms of Endearment**
   JANE ALEXANDER—Testament
   MERYL STREEP—Silkwood
   JULIE WALTERS—Educating Rita
   DEBRA WINGER—Terms of Endearment

SUPPORTING ACTOR

★ **JACK NICHOLSON—Terms of Endearment**
   CHARLES DURNING—To Be or Not to Be
   JOHN LITHGOW—Terms of Endearment
   SAM SHEPARD—The Right Stuff
   RIP TORN—Cross Creek

SUPPORTING ACTRESS

★ **LINDA HUNT—The Year of Living Dangerously**
   CHER—Silkwood
   GLENN CLOSE—The Big Chill
   AMY IRVING—Yentl
   ALFRE WOODARD—Cross Creek

DIRECTOR

★ **TERMS OF ENDEARMENT—James L. Brooks**
THE DRESSER—Peter Yates
FANNY AND ALEXANDER—Ingmar Bergman
SILKWOOD—Mike Nichols
TENDER MERCIES—Bruce Beresford

CINEMATOGRAPHY

★ **FANNY AND ALEXANDER—Sven Nykvist**
FLASHDANCE—Don Peterman
THE RIGHT STUFF—Caleb Deschanel
WARGAMES—William A. Fraker
ZELIG—Gordon Willis

VISUAL EFFECTS

★ **RETURN OF THE JEDI**

ART DIRECTION

★ **FANNY AND ALEXANDER**
RETURN OF THE JEDI
THE RIGHT STUFF
TERMS OF ENDEARMENT
YENTL

DRAMATIC SCORE

★ **THE RIGHT STUFF—Bill Conti**
CROSS CREEK—Leonard Rosenman
RETURN OF THE JEDI—John Williams
TERMS OF ENDEARMENT—Michael Gore
UNDER FIRE—Jerry Goldsmith

MUSICAL SCORE

★ **YENTL—Michel Legrand, Alan & Marilyn Bergman**
THE STING II—Lalo Schifrin
TRADING PLACES—Elmer Bernstein

SONG

★ **WHAT A FEELING** *from* **Flashdance**
MANIAC *from* Flashdance
OVER YOU *from* Tender Mercies
PAPA, CAN YOU HEAR ME? *from* Yentl
THE WAY HE MAKES ME FEEL *from* Yentl

1985

BEST PICTURE

★ **AMADEUS**
  THE KILLING FIELDS
  A PASSAGE TO INDIA
  PLACES IN THE HEART
  A SOLDIER'S STORY

ACTOR

★ **F. MURRAY ABRAHAM—Amadeus**
  JEFF BRIDGES—Starman
  ALBERT FINNEY—Under the Volcano
  TOM HULCE—Amadeus
  SAM WATERSTON—The Killing Fields

ACTRESS

★ **SALLY FIELD—Places in the Heart***
  JUDY DAVIS—A Passage to India
  JESSICA LANGE—Country
  VANESSA REDGRAVE—The Bostonians
  SISSY SPACEK—The River

SUPPORTING ACTOR

★ **HAING S. NGOR—The Killing Fields**
  ADOLPH CAESAR—A Soldier's Story
  JOHN MALKOVICH—Places in the Heart
  PAT MORITA—The Karate Kid
  RALPH RICHARDSON—Greystoke: The Legend of
      Tarzan, Lord of the Apes

SUPPORTING ACTRESS

★ **PEGGY ASHCROFT—A Passage to India**
  GLENN CLOSE—The Natural
  LINDSAY CROUSE—Places in the Heart
  CHRISTINE LAHTI—Swing Shift
  GERALDINE PAGE—The Pope of Greenwich Village

DIRECTOR

★ **AMADEUS—Miloš Forman**
BRADWAY DANNY ROSE—Woody Allen
THE KILLING FIELDS—Roland Joffé
A PASSAGE TO INDIA—David Lean
PLACES IN THE HEART—Robert Benton

CINEMATOGRAPHY

★ **THE KILLING FIELDS—Chris Menges**
AMADEUS—Miroslav Ondříček
THE NATURAL—Caleb Deschanel
A PASSAGE TO INDIA—Ernest Day
THE RIVER—Vilmos Zsigmond

VISUAL EFFECTS

★ **INDIANA JONES AND THE TEMPLE OF DOOM**
2010
GHOSTBUSTERS

ART DIRECTION

★ **AMADEUS**
2010
THE COTTON CLUB
THE NATURAL
A PASSAGE TO INDIA

DRAMATIC SCORE

★ **A PASSAGE TO INDIA—Maurice Jarre**
INDIANA JONES AND THE TEMPLE OF DOOM—John
    Williams
THE NATURAL—Randy Williams
THE RIVER—John Williams
UNDER THE VOLCANO—Alex North

MUSICAL SCORE

★ **PURPLE RAIN—Prince**
THE MUPPETS TAKE MANHATTAN—Jeff Moss
SONGWRITER—Kris Kristofferson

SONG

★ **I JUST CALLED TO SAY I LOVE YOU** *from* **The Woman
    in Red**
FOOTLOOSE *from* Footloose
GHOSTBUSTERS *from* Ghostbusters
LET'S HERE IT FOR THE BOY *from* Footloose
TAKE A LOOK AT ME NOW *from* Against All Odds

1986

*PURPLE *nominations: 11; wins: 0.*

BEST PICTURE

★ **OUT OF AFRICA**
THE COLOR PURPLE*
KISS OF THE SPIDER WOMAN
PRIZZI'S HONOR
WITNESS

ACTOR

★ **WILLIAM HURT—Kiss of the Spider Woman**
HARRISON FORD—Witness
JAMES GARNER—Murphy's Romance
JACK NICHOLSON—Prizzi's Honor
JON VOIGHT—Runaway Train

ACTRESS

★ **GERALDINE PAGE—The Trip to Bountiful**
ANNE BANCROFT—Agnes of God
WHOOPI GOLDBERG—The Color Purple*
JESSICA LANGE—Sweet Dreams
MERYL STREEP—Out of Africa

SUPPORTING ACTOR

★ **DON AMECHE—Cocoon**
KLAUS MARIA BRANDAUER—Out of Africa
WILLIAM HICKEY—Prizzi's Honor
ROBERT LOGGIA—Jagged Edge
ERIC ROBERTS—Runaway Train

SUPPORTING ACTRESS

★ **ANJELICA HUSTON—Prizzi's Honor**
MARGARET AVERY—The Color Purple*
AMY MADIGAN—Twice in a Lifetime
MEG TILLY—Agnes of God
OPRAH WINFREY—The Color Purple*

DIRECTOR

★ **OUT OF AFRICA—Sydney Pollack**
KISS OF THE SPIDER WOMAN—Héctor Babenco
PRIZZI'S HONOR—John Huston
RAN—Akira Kurosawa
WITNESS—Peter Weir

CINEMATOGRAPHY

★ **OUT OF AFRICA—David Watkin**
THE COLOR PURPLE—Allen Daviau*
MURPHY'S ROMANCE—William A. Fraker
RAN—Takao Saito, Masaharu Ueda, Asakazu Nakai
WITNESS—John Seale

ART DIRECTION

★ **OUT OF AFRICA**
BRAZIL
THE COLOR PURPLE*
RAN
WITNESS

VISUAL EFFECTS

★ **COCOON**
RETURN TO OZ
YOUNG SHERLOCK HOLMES

SCORE

★ **OUT OF AFRICA—John Barry**
AGNES OF GOD—Georges Delerue
THE COLOR PURPLE—Quincy Jones (& eleven others)*
SILVERADO—Bruce Broughton
WITNESS—Maurice Jarre

SONG

★ **SAY YOU, SAY ME** *from* **White Nights**
MISS CELIE'S BLUES (Sister) *from* The Color Purple*
THE POWER OF LOVE *from* Back to the Future
SEPARATE LIVES *from* White Nights
SURPRISE SURPRISE *from* A Chorus Line

Dorothy Chandler Pavilion, Los Angeles   March 24, 1986

1987

*Absentee Newman's prediction comes true:
"I've been there six times and lost. Maybe if I stay away, I'll win."*

BEST PICTURE

★ **PLATOON**
CHILDREN OF A LESSER GOD
HANNAH AND HER SISTERS
THE MISSION
A ROOM WITH A VIEW

ACTOR

★ **PAUL NEWMAN—The Color of Money***
DEXTER GORDON—Round Midnight
BOB HOSKINS—Mona Lisa
WILLIAM HURT—Children of a Lesser God
JAMES WOODS—Salvador

ACTRESS

★ **MARLEE MATLIN—Children of a Lesser God**
JANE FONDA—The Morning After
SISSY SPACEK—Crimes of the Heart
KATHLEEN TURNER—Peggy Sue Got Married
SIGOURNEY WEAVER—Aliens

SUPPORTING ACTOR

★ **MICHAEL CAINE—Hannah and Her Sisters**
TOM BERENGER—Platoon
WILLEM DAFOE—Platoon
DENHOLM ELLIOTT—A Room with a View
DENNIS HOPPER—Hoosiers

SUPPORTING ACTRESS

★ **DIANNE WIEST—Hannah and her Sisters**
TESS HARPER—Crimes of the Heart
PIPER LAURIE—Children of a Lesser God
MARY ELIZABETH MASTRANTONIO—The Color of Money
MAGGIE SMITH—A Room with a View

DIRECTOR

★ **PLATOON—Oliver Stone**
BLUE VELVET—David Llynch
HANNAH AND HER SISTERS—Woody Allen
THE MISSION—Roland Joffé
A ROOM WITH A VIEW—James Ivory

CINEMATOGRAPHY

★ **THE MISSION—Chris Menges**
PEGGY SUE GOT MARRIED—Jordan Cronenweth
PLATOON—Robert Richardson
A ROOM WITH A VIEW—Tony Pierce-Roberts
STAR TREK IV: THE VOYAGE HOME—Don Peterman

ART DIRECTION

★ **A ROOM WITH A VIEW**
ALIENS
THE COLOR OF MONEY
HANNAH AND HER SISTERS
THE MISSION

VISUAL EFFECTS

★ **ALIENS**
LITTLE SHOP OF HORRORS
POLTERGEIST II: THE OTHER SIDE

SCORE

★ **ROUND MIDNIGHT—Herbie Hancock**
ALIENS—James Horner
HOOSIERS—Jerry Goldsmith
THE MISSION—Ennio Morricone
STAR TREK IV: THE VOYAGE HOME—Leonard Rosenman

SONG

★ **TAKE MY BREATH AWAY** *from* **Top Gun**
GLORY OF LOVE *from* The Karate Kid Part II
LIFE IN A LOOKING GLASS *from* That's Life!
MEAN GREEN MOTHER FROM OUTER SPACE *from* Little
   Shop of Horrors
SOMEWHERE OUT THERE *from* An American Tail

1988

Ad libs by comedian presenters compensate for writers strike.

BEST PICTURE

★ **THE LAST EMPEROR**
BROADCAST NEWS
FATAL ATTRACTION
HOPE AND GLORY
MOONSTRUCK

ACTOR

★ **MICHAEL DOUGLAS—Wall Street**
WILLIAM HURT—Broadcast News
MARCELLO MASTROIANNI—Dark Eyes
JACK NICHOLSON—Ironweed
ROBIN WILLIAMS—Good Morning, Vietnam

ACTRESS

★ **CHER—Moonstruck**
GLENN CLOSE—Fatal Attraction
HOLLY HUNTER—Broadcast News
SALLY KIRKLAND—Anna
MERYL STREEP—Ironweed

SUPPORTING ACTOR

★ **SEAN CONNERY—The Untouchables**
ALBERT BROOKS—Broadcast News
MORGAN FREEMAN—Street Smart
VINCENT GARDENIA—Moonstruck
DENZEL WASHINGTON—Cry Freedom

SUPPORTING ACTRESS

★ **OLYMPIA DUKAKIS—Moonstruck**
NORMA ALEANDRO—Gaby: A True Story
ANNE ARCHER—Fatal Attraction
ANNE RAMSEY—Throw Momma from the Train
ANN SOTHERN—The Whales of August

DIRECTOR

★ **THE LAST EMPEROR—Bernardo Bertolucci**
FATAL ATTRACTION—Adrian Lyne
HOPE AND GLORY—John Boorman
MOONSTRUCK—Norman Jewison
MY LIFE AS A DOG—Lasse Hallström

CINEMATOGRAPHY

★ **THE LAST EMPEROR—Vittorio Storaro**
BROADCAST NEWS—Michael Ballhaus
EMPIRE OF THE SUN—Allen Daviau
HOPE AND GLORY—Philippe Rousselot
MATEWAN—Haskell Wexler

ART DIRECTION

★ **THE LAST EMPEROR**
EMPIRE OF THE SUN
HOPE AND GLORY
RADIO DAYS
THE UNTOUCHABLES

VISUAL EFFECTS

★ **INNERSPACE**
PREDATOR

SCORE

★ **THE LAST EMPEROR—David Byrne, Cong Su, Ryuichi Sakamoto**
CRY FREEDOM—George Fenton and Jonas Gwangwa
EMPIRE OF THE SUN—John Williams
THE UNTOUCHABLES—Ennio Morricone
THE WITCHES OF EASTWICK—John Williams

SONG

★ **(I've Had) THE TIME OF MY LIFE** *from* **Dirty Dancing**
CRY FREEDOM *from* Cry Freedom
NOTHING'S GONNA STOP US NOW *from* Mannequin
SHAKEDOWN *from* Beverly Hills Cop II
STORYBOOK LOVE *from* The Princess Bride

1989

Merv Griffin sings "Coconuts" and Rob Lowe dances with Snow White in 11-minute opening disaster.

BEST PICTURE

★ **RAIN MAN**
   THE ACCIDENTAL TOURIST
   DANGEROUS LIAISONS
   MISSISSIPPI BURNING
   WORKING GIRL

ACTOR

★ **DUSTIN HOFFMAN—Rain Man**
   GENE HACKMAN—Mississippi Burning
   TOM HANKS—Big
   EDWARD JAMES OLMOS—Stand and Deliver
   MAX VON SYDOW—Pelle the Conqueror

ACTRESS

★ **JODIE FOSTER—The Accused**
   GLENN CLOSE—Dangerous Liaisons
   MELANIE GRIFFITH—Working Girl
   MERYL STREEP—A Cry in the Dark
   SIGOURNEY WEAVER—Gorillas in the Mist

SUPPORTING ACTOR

★ **KEVIN KLINE—A Fish Called Wanda**
   ALEC GUINNESS—Little Dorrit
   MARTIN LANDAU—Tucker: The Man and His Dream
   RIVER PHOENIX—Running on Empty
   DEAN STOCKWELL—Married to the Mob

SUPPORTING ACTRESS

★ **GEENA DAVIS—The Accidental Tourist**
   JOAN CUSACK—Working Girl
   FRANCES McDORMAND—Mississippi Burning
   MICHELLE PFEIFFER—Dangerous Liaisons
   SIGOURNEY WEAVER—Working Girl

DIRECTOR

★ **RAIN MAN—Barry Levinson**
  A FISH CALLED WANDA—Charles Crichton
  THE LAST TEMPTATION OF CHRIST—Martin Scorsese
  MISSISSIPPI BURNING—Alan Parker
  WORKING GIRL—Mike Nichols

CINEMATOGRAPHY

★ **MISSISSIPPI BURNING—Peter Biziou**
  RAIN MAN—John Seale
  TEQUILA SUNRISE—Conrad Hall
  THE UNBEARABLE LIGHTNESS OF BEING—Sven Nykvist
  WHO FRAMED ROGER RABBIT—Dean Cundey

ART DIRECTION

★ **DANGEROUS LIAISONS**
  BEACHES
  RAIN MAN
  TUCKER: THE MAN AND HIS DREAM
  WHO FRAMED ROGER RABBIT

VISUAL EFFECTS

★ **WHO FRAMED ROGER RABBIT**
  DIE HARD
  WILLOW

SCORE

★ **THE MILAGRO BEANFIELD WAR—Dave Grusin**
  THE ACCIDENTAL TOURIST—John Williams
  DANGEROUS LIAISONS—George Fenton
  GORILLAS IN THE MIST—Maurice Jarre
  RAIN MAN—Hans Zimmer

SONG

★ **LET THE RIVER RUN** *from* **Working Girl**
  CALLING YOU *from* Bagdad Cafe
  TWO HEARTS *from* Buster

1990

Among the presenters is an animated Bugs Bunny.

BEST PICTURE

★ **DRIVING MISS DAISY**
BORN ON THE FOURTH OF JULY
DEAD POETS SOCIETY
FIELD OF DREAMS
MY LEFT FOOT

ACTOR

★ **DANIEL DAY-LEWIS—My Left Foot**
KENNETH BRANAGH—Henry V
TOM CRUISE—Born on the Fourth of July
MORGAN FREEMAN—Driving Miss Daisy
ROBIN WILLIAMS—Dead Poets Society

ACTRESS

★ **JESSICA TANDY—Driving Miss Daisy**
ISABELLE ADJANI—Camille Claudel
PAULINE COLLINS—Shirley Valentine
JESSICA LANGE—Music Box
MICHELLE PFEIFFER—The Fabulous Baker Boys

SUPPORTING ACTOR

★ **DENZEL WASHINGTON—Glory**
DANNY AIELLO—Do the Right Thing
DAN AYKROYD—Driving Miss Daisy
MARLON BRANDO—A Dry White Season
MARTIN LANDAU—Crimes and Misdemeanors

SUPPORTING ACTRESS

★ **BRENDA FRICKER—My Left Foot**
ANJELICA HUSTON—Enemies: A Love Story
LENA OLIN—Enemies: A Love Story
JULIA ROBERTS—Steel Magnolias
DIANNE WIEST—Parenthood

DIRECTOR

★ **BORN ON THE FOURTH OF JULY—Oliver Stone**
CRIMES AND MISDEMEANORS—Woody Allen
DEAD POET'S SOCIETY—Peter Weir
HENRY V—Kenneth Branagh
MY LEFT FOOT—Jim Sheridan

CINEMATOGRAPHY

★ **GLORY—Freddie Francis**
THE ABYSS—Mikael Salomon
BLAZE—Haskell Wexler
BORN ON THE FOURTH OF JULY—Robert Richardson
THE FABULOUS BAKER BOYS—Michael Ballhaus

ART DIRECTION

★ **BATMAN**
THE ABYSS
THE ADVENTURES OF BARON MUNCHAUSEN
DRIVING MISS DAISY
GLORY

VISUAL EFFECTS

★ **THE ABYSS**
THE ADVENTURES OF BARON MUNCHOUSEN
BACK TO THE FUTURE PART II

SCORE

★ **THE LITTLE MERMAID—Alan Menken**
BORN ON THE FOURTH OF JULY—John Williams
THE FABULOUS BAKER BOYS—Dave Grusin
FIELD OF DREAMS—James Homer
INDIANA JONES AND THE LAST CRUSADE—John Williams

SONG

★ **UNDER THE SEA** *from* **The Little Mermaid**
AFTER ALL *from* Chances Are
THE GIRL WHO USED TO BE ME *from* Shirley Valentine
I LOVE TO SEE YOU SMILE *from* Parenthood
KISS THE GIRL *from* The Little Mermaid

Dorothy Chandler Pavilion, Los Angeles   March 26, 1990

1991

First Oscars host to win Emmy.

BEST PICTURE

★ **DANCES WITH WOLVES**
  AWAKENINGS
  GHOST
  THE GODFATHER: PART III
  GOODFELLAS

ACTOR

★ **JEREMY IRONS—Reversal of Fortune**
  KEVIN COSTNER—Dances with Wolves
  ROBERT DE NIRO—Awakenings
  GÉRARD DEPARDIEU—Cyrano de Bergerac
  RICHARD HARRIS—The Field

ACTRESS

★ **KATHY BATES—Misery**
  ANJELICA HUSTON—The Grifters
  JULIA ROBERTS—Pretty Woman
  MERYL STREEP—Postcards from the Edge
  JOANNE WOODWARD—Mr. & Mrs. Bridge

SUPPORTING ACTOR

★ **JOE PESCI—Goodfellas**
  BRUCE DAVISON—Longtime Companion
  ANDY GARCIA—The Godfather: Part III
  GRAHAM GREENE—Dances with Wolves
  AL PACINO—Dick Tracy

SUPPORTING ACTRESS

★ **WHOOPI GOLDBERG—Ghost**
  ANNETTE BENING—The Grifters
  LORRAINE BRACCO—Goodfellas
  DIANE LADD—Wild at Heart
  MARY McDONNELL—Dances with Wolves

DIRECTOR

★ **DANCES WITH WOLVES—Kevin Costner**
THE GODFATHER PART III—Francis Ford Coppola
GOODFELLAS—Martin Scorsese
THE GRIFTERS—Stephen Frears
REVERSAL OF FORTUNE—Barbet Schroeder

CINEMATOGRAPHY

★ **DANCES WITH WOLVES—Dean Semler**
AVALON—Allen Daviau
DICK TRACY—Vittorio Storaro
THE GODFATHER PART III—Gordon Willis
HENRY & JUNE—Philippe Rousselot

ART DIRECTION

★ **DICK TRACY**
CYRANO DE BERGERAC
DANCES WITH WOLVES
THE GODFATHER PART III
HAMLET

VISUAL EFFECTS

★ **TOTAL RECALL**

SCORE

★ **DANCES WITH WOLVES—John Barry**
AVALON—Randy Newman
GHOST—Maurice Jarre
HAVANA—David Grusin
HOME ALONE—John Williams

SONG

★ **SOONER OR LATER** *from* **Dick Tracy**
BLAZE OF GLORY *from* Young Guns II
I'M CHECKIN' OUT *from* Postcards from the Edge
PROMISE ME YOU'LL REMEMBER *from* The Godfather
Part III
SOMEWHERE IN MY MEMORY *from* Home Alone

1992

During acceptance speech, Palance drops to floor, does one-arm push-ups.

BEST PICTURE

★ **THE SILENCE OF THE LAMBS**
 BEAUTY AND THE BEAST
 BUGSY
 JFK
 THE PRINCE OF TIDES

ACTOR

★ **ANTHONY HOPKINS—The Silence of the Lambs**
 WARREN BEATTY—Bugsy
 ROBERT DE NIRO—Cape Fear
 NICK NOLTE—The Prince of Tides
 ROBIN WILLIAMS—The Fisher King

ACTRESS

★ **JODIE FOSTER—The Silence of the Lambs**
 GEENA DAVIS—Thelma & Louise
 LAURA DERN—Rambling Rose
 BETTE MIDLER—For the Boys
 SUSAN SARANDON—Thelma & Louise

SUPPORTING ACTOR

★ **JACK PALANCE—City Slickers***
 TOMMY LEE JONES—JFK
 HARVEY KEITEL—Bugsy
 BEN KINGSLEY—Bugsy
 MICHAEL LERNER—Barton Fink

SUPPORTING ACTRESS

★ **MERCEDES RUEHL—The Fisher King**
 DIANE LADD—Rambling Rose
 JULIETTE LEWIS—Cape Fear
 KATE NELLIGAN—The Prince of Tides
 JESSICA TANDY—Fried Green Tomatoes

DIRECTOR

★ **THE SILENCE OF THE LAMBS—Jonathan Demme**
BOYZ N THE HOOD—John Singleton
BUGSY—Barry Livingston
JFK—Oliver Stone
THELMA & LOUISE—Ridley Scott

CINEMATOGRAPHY

★ **JFK—Robert Richardson**
BUGSY—Allen Daviau
THE PRINCE OF TIDES—Stephen Goldblatt
TERMINATOR 2: JUDGMENT DAY—Adam Greenberg
THELMA & LOUISE—Adrian Biddle

ART DIRECTION

★ **BUGSY**
BARTON FINK
THE FISHER KING
HOOK
THE PRINCE OF TIDES

VISUAL EFFECTS

★ **TERMINATOR 2: JUDGMENT DAY**
BACKDRAFT
HOOK

SCORE

★ **BEAUTY AND THE BEAST—Alan Menken**
BUGSY—Ennio Morricone
THE FISHER KING—George Fenton
JFK—John Williams
THE PRINCE OF TIDES—James Newton Howard

SONG

★ **BEAUTY AND THE BEAST** *from* **Beauty and the Beast**
BE OUR GUEST *from* Beauty and the Beast
BELLE *from* Beauty and the Beast
(Everything I do) I DO IT FOR YOU *from* Robin Hood:
    Prince of Thieves
WHEN YOU'RE ALONE *from* Hook

Dorothy Chandler Pavilion, Los Angeles   March 30, 1992

1993

*Elizabeth Taylor honored for work against AIDS;
all wear red ribbons.*

BEST PICTURE

★ **UNFORGIVEN**
THE CRYING GAME
A FEW GOOD MEN
HOWARDS END
SCENT OF A WOMAN

ACTOR

★ **AL PACINO—Scent of a Woman**
ROBERT DOWNEY JR.—Chaplin
CLINT EASTWOOD—Unforgiven
STEPHEN REA—The Crying Game
DENZEL WASHINGTON—Malcolm X

ACTRESS

★ **EMMA THOMPSON—Howards End**
CATHERINE DENEUVE—Indochine
MARY McDONNELL—Passion Fish
MICHELLE PFEIFFER—Love Field
SUSAN SARANDON—Lorenzo's Oil

SUPPORTING ACTOR

★ **GENE HACKMAN—Unforgiven**
JAYE DAVIDSON—The Crying Game
JACK NICHOLSON—A Few Good Men
AL PACINO—Glengarry Glen Ross
DAVID PAYMER—Mr. Saturday Night

SUPPORTING ACTRESS

★ **MARISA TOMEI—My Cousin Vinny**
JUDY DAVIS—Husbands and Wives
JOAN PLOWRIGHT—Enchanted April
VANESSA REDGRAVE—Howards End
MIRANDA RICHARDSON—Damage

DIRECTOR

★ **UNFORGIVEN—Clint Eastwood**
THE CRYING GAME—Neil Jordan
HOWARDS END—James Ivory
THE PLAYER—Robert Altman
SCENT OF A WOMAN—Martin Brest

CINEMATOGRAPHY

★ **A RIVER RUNS THROUGH IT—Philippe Rousselot**
HOFFA—Stephen H. Burum
HOWARDS END—Tony Pierce-Roberts
THE LOVER—Robert Fraisse
UNFORGIVEN—Jack N. Green

ART DIRECTION

★ **HOWARDS END**
BRAM STOKER'S DRACULA
CHAPLIN
TOYS
UNFORGIVEN

VISUAL EFFECTS

★ **DEATH BECOMES HER**
ALIEN³
BATMAN RETURNS

SCORE

★ **ALADDIN—Alan Menken**
BASIC INSTINCT—Jerry Goldsmith
CHAPLIN—John Barry
HOWARDS END—Richard Robbins
A RIVER RUNS THROUGH IT—Mark Isham

SONG

★ **A WHOLE NEW WORLD** *from* **Aladdin**
BEAUTIFUL MARIA OF MY SOUL *from* The Mambo Kings
FRIEND LIKE ME *from* Aladdin
I HAVE NOTHING *from* The Bodyguard
RUN TO YOU *from* The Bodyguard

1994

*In passionate speech, Hanks inadvertently
outs his high school drama teacher.*

BEST PICTURE

★ **SHINDLER'S LIST**
THE FUGITIVE
IN THE NAME OF THE FATHER
THE PIANO
THE REMAINS OF THE DAY

ACTOR

★ **TOM HANKS—Philadelphia***
DANIEL DAY-LEWIS—In the Name of the Father
LAURENCE FISHBURNE—What's Love Got to Do with It
ANTHONY HOPKINS—The Remains of the Day
LIAM NEESON—Schindler's List

ACTRESS

★ **HOLLY HUNTER—The Piano**
ANGELA BASSETT—What's Love Got to Do with It
STOCKARD CHANNING—Six Degrees of Separation
EMMA THOMPSON—The Remains of the Day
DEBRA WINGER—Shadowlands

SUPPORTING ACTOR

★ **TOMMY LEE JONES—The Fugitive**
LEONARDO DiCAPRIO—What's Eating Gilbert Grape
RALPH FIENNES—Schindler's List
JOHN MALKOVICH—In the Line of Fire
PETE POSTLETHWAITE—In the Name of the Father

SUPPORTING ACTRESS

★ **ANNA PAQUIN—The Piano**
HOLLY HUNTER—The Firm
ROSIE PEREZ—Fearless
WINONA RYDER—The Age of Innocence
EMMA THOMPSON—In the Name of the Father

DIRECTOR

★ **SCHINDLER'S LIST—Steven Speilberg**
IN THE NAME OF THE FATHER—Jim Sheridan
THE PIANO—Jane Campion
THE REMAINS OF THE DAY—James Ivory
SHORT CUTS—Robert Altman

CINEMATOGRAPHY

★ **SHINDLER'S LIST—Janusz Kamiński**
FAREWELL MY CONCUBINE—Gu Changwei
THE FUGITIVE—Michael Chapman
THE PIANO—Stuart Dryburgh
SEARCHING FOR BOBBY FISCHER—Conrad Hall

ART DIRECTION

★ **SHINDLER'S LIST**
ADDAMS FAMILY VALUES
THE AGE OF INNOCENCE
ORLANDO
THE REMAINS OF THE DAY

VISUAL EFFECTS

★ **JURASSIC PARK**
CLIFFHANGER
THE NIGHTMARE BEFORE CHRISTMAS

SCORE

★ **SHINDLER'S LIST—John Williams**
THE AGE OF INNOCENCE—Elmer Bernstein
THE FIRM—Dave Grusin
THE FUGITIVE—James Newton Howard
THE REMAINS OF THE DAY—Richard Robbins

SONG

★ **STREETS OF PHILADELPHIA** *from* **Philadelphia**
AGAIN *from* Poetic Justice
THE DAY I FALL IN LOVE *from* Beethoven's 2nd
PHILADELPHIA *from* Philadelphia
A WINK AND A SMILE *from* Sleepless in Seattle

Dorothy Chandler Pavilion, Los Angeles   March 21, 1994

1995

BEST PICTURE

★ **FORREST GUMP**
FOUR WEDDINGS AND A FUNERAL
PULP FICTION
QUIZ SHOW
THE SHAWSHANK REDEMPTION

ACTOR

★ **TOM HANKS—Forest Gump**
MORGAN FREEMAN—The Shawshank Redemption
NIGEL HAWTHORNE—The Madness of King George
PAUL NEWMAN—Nobody's Fool
JOHN TRAVOLTA—Pulp Fiction

ACTRESS

★ **JESSICA LANGE—Blue Sky**
JODIE FOSTER—Nell
MIRANDA RICHARDSON—Tom & Viv
WINONA RYDER—Little Women
SUSAN SARANDON—The Client

SUPPORTING ACTOR

★ **MARTIN LANDAU—Ed Wood**
SAMUEL L. JACKSON—Pulp Fiction
CHAZZ PALMINTERI—Bullets Over Broadway
PAUL SCOFIELD—Quiz Show
GARY SINISE—Forrest Gump

SUPPORTING ACTRESS

★ **DIANNE WIEST—Bullets Over Broadway**
ROSEMARY HARRIS—Tom & Viv
HELEN MIRREN—The Madness of King George
UMA THURMAN—Pulp Fiction
JENNIFER TILLY—Bullets Over Broadway

DIRECTOR

★ **FORREST GUMP—Robert Zemeckis**
BULLETS OVER BROADWAY—Woody Allen
PULP FICTION—Quentin Tarantino
QUIZ SHOW—Robert Redford
THREE COLORS: RED—Krzysztof Kieślowski

CINEMATOGRAPHY

★ **LEGENDS OF THE FALL—John Toll**
FORREST GUMP—Don Burgess
THE SHAWSHANK REDEMPTION—Roger Deakins
THREE COLORS: RED—Pioitr Sobicinski
WYATT EARP—Owen Roizman

ART DIRECTION

★ **THE MADNESS OF KING GEORGE**
BULLETS OVER BROADWAY
FORREST GUMP
INTERVIEW WITH THE VAMPIRE
LEGENDS OF THE FALL

VISUAL EFFECTS

★ **FOREST GUMP**
THE MASK
TRUE LIES

SCORE

★ **THE LION KING—Hans Zimmer**
FORREST GUMP—Alan Silvestri
INTERVIEW WITH THE VAMPIRE—Elliot Goldenthal
LITTLE WOMEN—Thomas Newman
THE SHAWSHANK REDEMPTION—Thomas Newman

SONG

★ **CAN YOU FEEL THE LOVE TONIGHT** *from* **The Lion King**
CIRCLE OF LIFE *from* The Lion King
HAKUNA MATATA *from* The Lion King
LOOK WHAT LOVE HAS DONE *from* Junior
MAKE UP YOUR MIND *from* The Paper

1996

Surprise appearance by Christopher Reeve, paralyzed from equestrian accident, brings extended ovation (and few dry eyes).

BEST PICTURE

★ **BRAVEHEART**
APOLLO 13
BABE
IL POSTINO: THE POSTMAN
SENSE AND SENSIBILITY

ACTOR

★ **NICOLAS CAGE—Leaving Las Vegas**
RICHARD DREYFUSS—Mr. Holland's Opus
ANTHONY HOPKINS—Nixon
SEAN PENN—Dead Man Walking
MASSIMO TROISI—Il Postino: The Postman

ACTRESS

★ **SUSAN SARANDON—Dead Man Walking**
ELISABETH SHUE—Leaving Las Vegas
SHARON STONE—Casino
MERYL STREEP—The Bridges of Madison County
EMMA THOMPSON—Sense and Sensibility

SUPPORTING ACTOR

★ **KEVIN SPACEY—The Usual Suspects**
JAMES CROMWELL—Babe
ED HARRIS—Apollo 13
BRAD PITT—Twelve Monkeys
TIM ROTH—Rob Roy

SUPPORTING ACTRESS

★ **MIRA SORVINO—Mighty Aphrodite**
JOAN ALLEN—Nixon
KATHLEEN QUINLAN—Apollo 13
MARE WINNINGHAM—Georgia
KATE WINSLET—Sense and Sensibility

DIRECTOR

★ **BRAVEHEART—Mel Gibson**
BABE—Chris Noonan
DEAD MAN WALKING—Tim Robbins
LEAVING LAS VEGAS—Mike Figgis
IL POSTINO: THE POSTMAN—Michael Radford

CINEMATOGRAPHY

★ **BRAVEHEART—John Toll**
BATMAN FOREVER—Stephen Goldblatt
A LITTLE PRINCESS-Emmanuel Lubezki
SENSE AND SENSIBILITY—Michael Coulter
SHANGHAI TRIAD—Lu Yue

VISUAL EFFECTS

★ **BABE**
APOLLO 13

DRAMATIC SCORE

★ **IL POSTINO: THE POSTMAN—Luis Enriquez Bacalov**
APOLLO 13—James Horner
BRAVEHEART—James Horner
NIXON—John Williams
SENSE AND SENSIBILITY—Patrick Doyle

MUSICAL OR COMEDY SCORE

★ **POCAHONTAS—Alan Menken and Stephen Schwartz**
THE AMERICAN PRESIDENT—Marc Shaiman
SABRINA—John Williams
TOY STORY—Randy Newman
UNSTRUNG HEROES—Thomas Newman

SONG

★ **COLORS OF THE WIND** *from* **Pocahontas**
DEAD MAN WALKIN' *from* Dead Man Walking
HAVE YOU EVER REALLY LOVED A WOMAN *from* Don
   Juan DeMarco
MOONLIGHT *from* Sabrina
YOU'VE GOT A FRIEND IN ME *from* Toy Story

1997

Muhammad Ali-George Foreman bout documentary wins Oscar; both fighters appear on stage, Ali suffering from Parkinson's.

BEST PICTURE

★ **THE ENGLISH PATIENT**
FARGO
JERRY MAGUIRE
SECRETS & LIES
SHINE

ACTOR

★ **GEOFFREY RUSH—Shine**
TOM CRUISE—Jerry Maguire
RALPH FIENNES—The English Patient
WOODY HARRELSON—The People vs. Larry Flynt
BILLY BOB THORNTON—Sling Blade

ACTRESS

★ **FRANCES McDORMAND—Fargo**
BRENDA BLETHYN—Secrets & Lies
DIANE KEATON—Marvin's Room
KRISTIN SCOTT THOMAS—The English Patient
EMILY WATSON—Breaking the Waves

SUPPORTING ACTOR

★ **CUBA GOODING JR.—Jerry Maguire**
WILLIAM H. MACY—Fargo
ARMIN MUELLER-STAHL—Shine
EDWARD NORTON—Primal Fear
JAMES WOODS—Ghosts of Mississippi

SUPPORTING ACTRESS

★ **JULIETTE BINOCHE—The English Patient**
JOAN ALLEN—The Crucible
LAUREN BACALL—The Mirror Has Two Faces
BARBARA HERSHEY—The Portrait of a Lady
MARIANNE JEAN-BAPTISTE—Secrets & Lies

DIRECTOR

★ **THE ENGLISH PATIENT—Anthony Minghella**
FARGO—Joel Coen
THE PEOPLE VS. LARRY FLYNT—Miloš Forman
SECRETS & LIES—Mike Leigh
SHINE—Scott Hicks

CINEMATOGRAPHY

★ **THE ENGLISH PATIENT—John Seale**
EVITA—Darius Khondji
FARGO—Roger Deakins
FLY AWAY HOME—Caleb Menges
MICHAEL COLLINS—Chris Menges

VISUAL EFFECTS

★ **INDEPENDENCE DAY**
DRAGONHEART
TWISTER

DRAMATIC SCORE

★ **THE ENGLISH PATIENT—Gabriel Yared**
HAMLET—Patrick Doyle
MICHAEL COLLINS—Elliot Goldenthal
SHINE—David Hirschfelder
SLEEPERS—John Williams

MUSICAL OR COMEDY SCORE

★ **EMMA—Rachel Portman**
THE FIRST WIVES CLUB—Marc Shaiman
THE HUNCHBACK OF NOTRE DAME—Alan Menken and
    Stephen Schwartz
JAMES AND THE GIANT PEACH—Randy Newman
THE PREACHER'S WIFE—Hans Zimmer

SONG

★ **YOU MUST LOVE ME** *from* **Evita**
BECAUSE YOU LOVED ME *from* Up Close & Personal
FOR THE FIRST TIME *from* One Fine Day
I FINALLY FOUND SOMEONE *from* The Mirror Has Two
    Faces
THAT THING YOU DO! *from* That Thing You Do!

1998

Crystal's second Emmy win as Oscars host.

BEST PICTURE

★ **TITANIC**
AS GOOD AS IT GETS
THE FULL MONTY
GOOD WILL HUNTING
L.A. CONFIDENTIAL

ACTOR

★ **JACK NICHOLSON—As Good as it Gets**
MATT DAMON—Good Will Hunting
ROBERT DUVALL—The Apostle
PETER FONDA—Ulee's Gold
DUSTIN HOFFMAN—Wag the Dog

ACTRESS

★ **HELEN HUNT—As Good as It Gets**
HELENA BONHAM CARTER—The Wings of the Dove
JULIE CHRISTIE—Afterglow
JUDI DENCH—Mrs. Brown
KATE WINSLET—Titanic

SUPPORTING ACTOR

★ **ROBIN WILLIAMS—Good Will Hunting**
ROBERT FORSTER—Jackie Brown
ANTHONY HOPKINS—Amistad
GREG KINNEAR—As Good as It Gets
BURT REYNOLDS—Boogie Nights

SUPPORTING ACTRESS

★ **KIM BASINGER—L.A. Confidential**
JOAN CUSACK—In & Out
MINNIE DRIVER—Good Will Hunting
JULIANNE MOORE—Boogie Nights
GLORIA STUART—Titanic

DIRECTOR

★ **TITANIC—James Cameron**
 THE FULL MONTY—Peter Cattaneo
 GOOD WILL HUNTING—Gus Van Sant
 L.A. CONFIDENTIAL—Curtis Hanson
 THE SWEET HEREAFTER—Atom Egoyan

CINEMATOGRAPHY

★ **TITANIC—Russell Carpenter**
 AMISTAD—Janusz Kamiński
 KUNDUN—Roger Deakins
 L.A. CONFIDENTIAL—Dante Spinotti
 THE WINGS OF THE DOVE—Eduardo Serra

VISUAL EFFECTS

★ **TITANIC**
 THE LOST WORLD: JURASSIC PARK
 STARSHIP TROOPERS

DRAMATIC SCORE

★ **TITANIC—James Horner**
 AMISTAD—John Williams
 GOOD WILL HUNTING—Danny Elfman
 KUNDUN—Philip Glass
 L.A. CONFIDENTIAL—Jerry Goldsmith

MUSICAL OR COMEDY SCORE

★ **THE FULL MONTY—Anne Dudley**
 ANASTASIA—Stephen Flaherty, Lynn Ahrens, David
  Newman
 AS GOOD AS IT GETS—Hans Zimmer
 MEN IN BLACK—Danny Elfman
 MY BEST FRIEND'S WEDDING—James Newton Howard

SONG

★ **MY HEART WILL GO ON** *from* **Titanic**
 GO THE DISTANCE *from* Hercules
 HOW DO I LIVE *from* Con Air
 JOURNEY TO THE PAST *from* Anastasia
 MISS MISERY *from* GOOD WILL HUNTING

1999

Michael Jackson buys 1940 Best Picture Oscar statuette for GONE WITH THE WIND *at Sotheby's for $1.54 million.*

BEST PICTURE

★ **SHAKESPEARE IN LOVE**
ELIZABETH
LIFE IS BEAUTIFUL
SAVING PRIVATE RYAN
THE THIN RED LINE

ACTOR

★ **ROBERTO BENIGNI—Life Is Beautiful**
TOM HANKS—Saving Private Ryan
IAN McKELLEN—Gods and Monsters
NICK NOLTE—Afflliction
EDWARD NORTON—American History X

ACTRESS

★ **GWYNETH PALTROW—Shakespeare in Love**
CATE BLANCHETT—Elizabeth
FERNANDA MONTENEGRO—Central Station
MERYL STREEP—One True Thing
EMILY WATSON—Hilary and Jackie

SUPPORTING ACTOR

★ **JAMES COBURN—Affliction**
ROBERT DUVALL—A Civil Action
ED HARRIS—The Truman Show
GEOFFREY RUSH—Shakespeare in Love
BILLY BOB THORNTON—A Simple Plan

SUPPORTING ACTRESS

★ **JUDI DENCH—Shakespeare in Love**
KATHY BATES—Primary Colors
BRENDA BLETHYN—Little Voice
RACHEL GRIFFITHS—Hilary and Jackie
LYNN REDGRAVE—Gods and Monsters

DIRECTOR

★ **SAVING PRIVATE RYAN—Steven Spielberg**
LIFE IS BEAUTIFUL—Roberto Benigni
SHAKESPEARE IN LOVE—John Madden
THE THIN RED LINE—Terrence Malick
THE TRUMAN SHOW—Peter Weir

CINEMATOGRAPHY

★ **SAVING PRIVATE RYAN—Janusz Kamiński**
A CIVIL ACTION—Conrad Hall
ELIZABETH—Remi Adefarasin
SHAKESPEARE IN LOVE—Richard Greatrex
THE THIN RED LINE—John Toll

VISUAL EFFECTS

★ **WHAT DREAMS MAY COME**
ARMAGEDDON
MIGHTY JOE YOUNG

DRAMATIC SCORE

★ **LIFE IS BEAUTIFUL—Nicola Piovani**
ELIZABETH—David Hirschfelder
PLEASANTVILLE—Randy Newman
SAVING PRIVATE RYAN—John Williams
THE THIN RED LINE—Hans Zimmer

MUSICAL OR COMEDY SCORE

★ **SHAKESPEARE IN LOVE—Stephen Warbeck**
A BUG'S LIFE—Randy Newman
MULAN—Matthew Wilder, David Zippel, Jerry Goldsmith
PATCH ADAMS—Marc Shaiman
THE PRINCE OF EGYPT—Stephen Schwartz and Hans
  Zimmer

SONG

★ **WHEN YOU BELIEVE** *from* **The Prince of Egypt**
I DON'T WANT TO MISS A THING *from* Armageddon THE
PRAYER *from* Quest for Camelot
A SOFT PLACE TO FALL *from* The Horse Whisperer
THAT'LL DO *from* Babe: Pig in the City

2000

Mislabeled US mail bags reveal 4,000 lost Academy voter ballots;
Koreatown, LA, Food-4-less trash bin produces 55 stolen Oscar statuettes.

BEST PICTURE

★ **AMERICAN BEAUTY**
  THE CIDER HOUSE RULES
  THE GREEN MILE
  THE INSIDER
  THE SIXTH SENSE

ACTOR

★ **KEVIN SPACEY—American Beauty**
  RUSSELL CROWE—The Insider
  RICHARD FARNSWORTH—The Straight Story
  SEAN PENN—Sweet and Lowdown
  DENZEL WASHINGTON—The Hurricane

ACTRESS

★ **HILARY SWANK—Boys Don't Cry**
  ANNETTE BENING—American Beauty
  JANET McTEER—Tumbleweeds
  JULIANNE MOORE—The End of the Affair
  MERYL STREEP—Music of the Heart

SUPPORTING ACTOR

★ **MICHAEL CAINE—The Cider House Rules**
  TOM CRUISE—Magnolia
  MICHAEL CLARKE DUNCAN—The Green Mile
  JUDE LAW—The Talented Mr. Ripley
  HALEY JOEL OSMENT—The Sixth Sense

SUPPORTING ACTRESS

★ **ANGELINA JOLIE—Girl, Interrupted**
  TONI COLLETTE—The Sixth Sense
  CATHERINE KEENER—Being John Malkovich
  SAMANTHA MORTON—Sweet and Lowdown
  CHLOË SEVIGNY—Boys Don't Cry

DIRECTOR

★ **AMERICAN BEAUTY—Sam Mendes**
BEING JOHN MALKOVICH—Spike Jonze
THE CIDER HOUSE RULES—Lasse Hallström
THE INSIDER—Michael Mann
THE SIXTH SENSE—M. Night Shyamalan

CINEMATOGRAPHY

★ **AMERICAN BEAUTY—Conrad Hall**
THE END OF THE AFFAIR—Roger Pratt
THE INSIDER—Dante Spinotti
SLEEPY HOLLOW—Emmanuel Lubezki
SNOW FALLING ON CEDARS—Robert Richardson

FILM EDITING

★ **THE MATRIX**
AMERICAN BEAUTY
THE CIDER HOUSE RULES
THE INSIDER
THE SIXTH SENSE

VISUAL EFFECTS

★ **THE MATRIX**
STAR WARS: EPISODE I: THE PHANTOM MENACE
STUART LITTLE

SCORE

★ **THE RED VIOLIN—John Corigliano**
AMERICAN BEAUTY—Thomas Newman
ANGELA'S ASHES—John Williams
THE CIDER HOUSE RULES—Rachel Portman
THE TALENTED MR. RIPLEY—Gabriel Yared

SONG

★ **YOU'LL BE IN MY HEART** *from* **Tarzan**
BLAME CANADA *from* South Park: Bigger, Longer, & Uncut
MUSIC OF MY HEART *from* Music of the Heart
SAVE ME *from* Magnolia
WHEN SHE LOVED ME *from* Toy Story 2

2001

Aunt Julia follows neice Emma's advice to wear "skunk dress."

BEST PICTURE

★ **GLADIATOR**
CHOCOLAT
CROUCHING TIGER, HIDDEN DRAGON
ERIN BROCKOVICH
TRAFFIC

ACTOR

★ **RUSSILL CROWE—Gladiator**
JAVIER BARDEM—Before Night Falls
TOM HANKS—Cast Away
ED HARRIS—Pollock
GEOFFREY RUSH—Quills

ACTRESS

★ **JULIA ROBERTS—Erin Brockovich***
JOAN ALLEN—The Contender
JULIETTE BINOCHE—Chocolat
ELLEN BURSTYN—Requiem for a Dream
LAURA LINNEY—You Can Count on Me

SUPPORTING ACTOR

★ **BENICIO DEL TORO—Traffic**
JEFF BRIDGES—The Contender
WILLEM DAFOE—Shadow of the Vampire
ALBERT FINNEY—Erin Brockovich
JOAQUIN PHOENIX—Gladiator

SUPPORTING ACTRESS

★ **MARCIA GAY HARDEN—Pollock**
JUDI DENCH—Chocolat
KATE HUDSON—Almost Famous
FRANCES McDORMAND—Almost Famous
JULIE WALTERS—Billy Elliot

DIRECTOR

★ **TRAFFIC—Steven Soderbergh**
BILLY ELLIOT—Stephen Daldry
CROUCHING TIGER, HIDDEN DRAGON—Ang Lee
ERIN BROCKOVICH—Stephen Soderbergh
GLADIATOR—Ridley Scott

CINEMATOGRAPHY

★ **CROUCHING TIGER, HIDDEN DRAGON—Peter Pau**
GLADIATOR—John Mathieson
MALÈNA—Lajos Koltai
O BROTHER, WHERE ART THOU?—Roger Deakins
THE PATRIOT—Caleb Deschanel

FILM EDITING

★ **TRAFFIC**
ALMOST FAMOUS
CROUCHING TIGER, HIDDEN DRAGON
GLADIATOR
WONDER BOYS

VISUAL EFFECTS

★ **GLADIATOR**
HOLLOW MAN
THE PERFECT STORM

SCORE

★ **CROUCHING TIGER, HIDDEN DRAGON—Tan Dun**
CHOCOLAT—Rachel Portman
GLADIATOR—Hans Zimmer
MALÈNA—Ennio Morricone
THE PATRIOT—John Williams

SONG

★ **THINGS HAVE CHANGED** *from* **Wonder Boys**
A FOOL IN LOVE *from* Meet the Parents
I'VE SEEN IT ALL *from* Dancer in the Dark
A LOVE BEFORE TIME *from* Crouching Tiger, Hidden
Dragon
MY FUNNY FRIEND AND ME *from* The Emperor's New
Groove

2002

Longest show in Oscar history (4 hrs 23 min).

Woody Allen urges filmakers to work in New York despite 9/11 attack.

BEST PICTURE

★ **A BEAUTIFUL MIND**
  GOSFORD PARK
  IN THE BEDROOM
  THE LORD OF THE RINGS: THE FELLOWSHIP OF THE RING
  MOULIN ROUGE!

ACTOR

★ **DENZEL WASHINGTON—Training Day**
  RUSSELL CROWE—A Beautiful Mind
  SEAN PENN—I Am Sam
  WILL SMITH—Ali
  TOM WILKINSON—In the Bedroom

ACTRESS

★ **HALLE BERRY—Monster's Ball**
  JUDI DENCH—Iris
  NICOLE KIDMAN—Moulin Rouge!
  SISSY SPACEK—In the Bedroom
  RENÉE ZELLWEGER—Bridget Jones's Diary

SUPPORTING ACTOR

★ **JIM BROADBENT—Iris**
  ETHAN HAWKE—Training Day
  BEN KINGSLEY—Sexy Beast
  IAN McKELLEN—The Lord of the Rings: The Fellowship
    of the Ring
  JON VOIGHT—Ali

SUPPORTING ACTRESS

★ **JENNIFER CONNELLY—A Beautiful Mind**
  HELEN MIRREN—Gosford Park
  MAGGIE SMITH—Gosford Park
  MARISA TOMEI—In the Bedroom
  KATE WINSLET—Iris

DIRECTOR

★ **A BEAUTIFUL MIND—Ron Howard**
BLACK HAWK DOWN—Ridlay Scott
GOSFORD PARK—Robert Altman
THE LORD OF THE RINGS: THE FELLOWSHIP OF THE RING
—Peter Jackson
MULHOLLAND DR.—David Lynch

CINEMATOGRAPHY

★ **THE LORD OF THE RINGS: THE FELLOWSHIP OF THE RING—Andrew Lesnie**
AMÉLIE—Bruno Delbonnel
BLACK HAWK DOWN—Slawomir Idziak
THE MAN WHO WASN'T THERE—Roger Deakins
MOULIN ROUGE!—Donald M. McAlpine

SCORE

★ **THE LORD OF THE RINGS: THE FELLOWSHIP OF THE RING—Howard Shore**
A.I. ARTIFICIAL INTELLIGENCE—John Williams
A BEAUTIFUL MIND—James Horner
HARRY POTTER AND THE SORCERER'S STONE—John Williams
MONSTERS, INC.—Randy Newman

SONG

★ **IF I DIDN'T HAVE YOU** *from* **Monsters, Inc.**
MAY IT BE *from* The Lord of the Rings: The Felloship of the Ring
THERE YOU'LL BE *from* Pearl Harbor
UNTIL... *from* Kate & Leopold
VANILLA SKY *from* Vanilla Sky

VISUAL EFFECTS

★ **THE LORD OF THE RINGS: THE FELLOWSHIP OF THE RING**
A.I. ARTIFICIAL INTELLIGENCE
PEARL HARBOR

ANIMATED FILM

★ **SHREK**
JIMMY NEUTRON: BOY GENIUS
MONSTERS, INC.

2003

*Invasion of Iraq sparks boycotts, protests,
and production curtailments.*

BEST PICTURE

★ **CHICAGO**
GANGS OF NEW YORK
THE HOURS
THE LORD OF THE RINGS: THE TWO TOWERS
THE PIANIST

ACTOR

★ **ADRIEN BRODY—The Pianist**
NICOLAS CAGE—Adaptation
MICHAEL CAINE—The Quiet American
DANIEL DAY-LEWIS—Gangs of New York
JACK NICHOLSON—About Schmidt

ACTRESS

★ **NICOLE KIDMAN—The Hours**
SALMA HAYEK—Frida
DIANE LANE—Unfaithful
JULIANNE MOORE—Far from Heaven
RENÉE ZELLWEGER—Chicago

SUPPORTING ACTOR

★ **CHRIS COOPER—Adaptation**
ED HARRIS—The Hours
PAUL NEWMAN—Road to Perdition
JOHN C. REILLY—Chicago
CHRISTOPHER WALKEN—Catch Me If You Can

SUPPORTING ACTRESS

★ **CATHERINE ZETA-JONES—Chicago**
KATHY BATES—About Schmidt
QUEEN LATIFAH—Chicago
JULIANNE MOORE—The Hours
MERYL STREEP—Adaptation

DIRECTOR

★ **THE PIANIST—Roman Polanski**
CHICAGO—Rob Marshall
GANGS OF NEW YORK—Martin Scorsese
THE HOURS—Stephen Daldry
TALK TO HER—Pedro Almodóvar

CINEMATOGRAPHY

★ **ROAD TO PERDITION—Conrad Hall**
CHICAGO—Dion Beebe
FAR FROM HEAVEN—Edward Lachman
GANGS OF NEW YORK—Michael Ballhaus
THE PIANIST—Paweł Edelman

SCORE

★ **FRIDA—Elliot Goldenthal**
CATCH ME IF YOU CAN—John Williams
FAR FROM HEAVEN—Elmer Bernstein
THE HOURS—Philip Glass
ROAD TO PERDITION—Thomas Newman

SONG

★ **LOSE YOURSELF** *from* **8 Mile**
BURN IT BLUE *from* Frida
FATHER AND DAUGHTER *from* The Wild Thornberrys Movie
THE HANDS THAT BUILT AMERICA *from* Gangs of New York
I MOVE ON *from* Chicago

VISUAL EFFECTS

★ **THE LORD OF THE RINGS: THE TWO TOWERS**
SPIDER-MAN
STAR WARS EPISODE II: ATTACK OF THE CLONES

ANIMATED FILM

★ **SPIRITED AWAY**
ICE AGE
LILO & STICH
SPIRIT STALLION OF THE CIMARRON
TREASURE PLANET

2004

Super Bowl halftime "wardrobe malfunction"
gives rise to Oscar 5-second tape delay.

BEST PICTURE

★ **THE LORD OF THE RINGS: THE RETURN OF THE KING**
LOST IN TRANSLATION
MASTER AND COMMANDER: THE FAR SIDE OF THE WORLD
MYSTIC RIVER
SEABISCUIT

ACTOR

★ **SEAN PENN—Mystic River**
JOHNNY DEPP—Pirates of the Caribbean: The Curse of the Black Pearl
BEN KINGSLEY—House of Sand and Fog
JUDE LAW—Cold Mountain
BILL MURRAY—Lost in Translation

ACTRESS

★ **CHARLIZE THERON—Monster**
KEISHA CASTLE-HUGHES—Whale Rider
DIANE KEATON—Something's Gotta Give
SAMANTHA MORTON—In America
NAOMI WATTS—21 Grams

SUPPORTING ACTOR

★ **TIM ROBBINS—Mystic River**
ALEC BALDWIN—The Cooler
BENICIO DEL TORO—21 Grams
DJIMON HOUNSOU—In America
KEN WATANABE—The Last Samurai

SUPPORTING ACTRESS

★ **RENÉE ZELLWEGER—Cold Mountain**
SHOHREH AGHDASHLOO—House of Sand and Fog
PATRICIA CLARKSON—Pieces of April
MARCIA GAY HARDEN—Mystic River
HOLLY HUNTER—Thirteen

DIRECTOR

★ **THE LORD OF THE RINGS: THE RETURN OF THE KING
—Peter Jackson**
CITY OF GOD—Fernando Meirelles
LOST IN TRANSLATION—Sofia Coppola
MASTER AND COMMANDER: THE FAR SIDE OF THE WORLD
—Peter Weir
MYSTIC RIVER—Clint Eastwood

CINEMATOGPHAPHY

★ **MASTER AND COMMANDER: THE FAR SIDE OF THE
WORLD—Russell Boyd**
CITY OF GOD—Cesar Charlone
COLD MOUNTAIN—John Seale
GIRL WITH A PEARL EARRING—Eduardo Serra
SEABISCUIT—John Schwartzman

SCORE

★ **THE LORD OF THE RINGS: THE RETURN OF THE KING
—Howard Shore**
BIG FISH—Danny Elfman
COLD MOUNTAIN—Gabriel Yared
FINDING NEMO—Thomas Newman
HOUSE OF SAND AND FOG—James Horner

SONG

★ **INTO THE WEST** *from* **The Lord of the Rings: The
Return of the King**
BELLEVILLE RENDEZ-VOUS *from* The Triplets of Belleville
A KISS AT THE END OF THE RAINBOW *from* A Mighty Wind
SCARLET TIDE *from* Cold Mountain
YOU WILL BE MY AIN TRUE LOVE *from* Cold Mountain

VISUAL EFFECTS

★ **THE LORD OF THE RINGS: THE RETURN OF THE KING**
MASTER AND COMMANDER: THE FAR SIDE OF THE WORLD
PIRATES OF THE CARIBBEAN: THE CURSE OF THE BLACK
PEARL

ANIMATED FILM

★ **FINDING NEMO**
BROTHER BEAR
THE TRIPLETS OF BELLEVILLE

2005

At 74, Eastwood oldest Oscar winning director.

BEST PICTURE

★ **MILLION DOLLAR BABY**
  THE AVIATOR
  FINDING NEVERLAND
  RAY
  SIDEWAYS

ACTOR

★ **JAMIE FOXX—Ray**
  DON CHEADLE—Hotel Rwanda
  JOHNNY DEPP—Finding Neverland
  LEONARDO DiCAPRIO—The Aviator
  CLINT EASTWOOD—Million Dollar Baby

ACTRESS

★ **HILARY SWANK—Million Dollar Baby**
  ANNETTE BENING—Being Julia
  CATALINA SANDINO MORENO—Maria Full of Grace
  IMELDA STAUNTON—Vera Drake
  KATE WINSLET—Eternal Sunshine of the Spotless Mind

SUPPORTING ACTOR

★ **MORGAN FREEMAN—Million Dollar Baby**
  ALAN ALDA—The Aviator
  THOMAS HADEN CHURCH—Sideways
  JAMIE FOXX—Collateral
  CLIVE OWEN—Closer

SUPPORTING ACTRESS

★ **CATE BLANCHETT—The Aviator**
  LAURA LINNEY—Kinsey
  VIRGINIA MADSEN—Sideways
  SOPHIE OKONEDO—Hotel Rwanda
  NATALIE PORTMAN—Closer

DIRECTOR

★ **MILLION DOLLAR BABY—Clint Eastwood***
  THE AVIATOR—Martin Scorsese
  RAY—Taylor Hackford
  SIDEWAYS—Alexander Payne
  VERA DRAKE—Mike Leigh

CINEMATOGPHAPHY

★ **THE AVIATOR—Robert Richardson**
  HOUSE OF FLYING DAGGERS—Zhao Xiaoding
  THE PASSION OF THE CHRIST—Caleb Deschanel
  THE PHANTOM OF THE OPERA—John Mathieson
  A VERY LONG ENGAGEMENT—Bruno Delbonnel

SCORE

★ **FINDING NEVERLAND—Jan A.P. Kaczmarek**
  HARRY POTTER AND THE PRISONER OF AZKABAN—John
    Williams
  LEMONY SNICKET'S A SERIES OF UNFORTUNATE EVENTS—
    Thomas Newman
  THE PASSION OF THE CHRIST—John Debney
  THE VILLAGE—James Newton Howard

SONG

★ **AL OTRO LADO DEL RIO** *from* **The Motorcycle Diaries**
  ACCIDENTALLY IN LOVE *from* Shrek 2
  BELIEVE *from* The Polar Express
  LEARN TO BE LONELY *from* The Phantom of the Opera
  LOOK TO YOUR PATH *from* The Chorus

VISUAL EFFECTS

★ **SPIDER-MAN 2**
  HARRY POTTER AND THE PRISONER OF AZKABAN
  I, ROBOT

ANIMATED FILM

★ **THE INCREDIBLES**
  SHARK TALE
  SHREK 2

2006

First rap song performed at Oscars.

BEST PICTURE

★ **CRASH**
BROKEBACK MOUNTAIN
CAPOTE
GOOD NIGHT, AND GOOD LUCK
MUNICH

ACTOR

★ **PHILIP SEYMOUR HOFFMAN—Capote**
TERRENCE HOWARD—Hustle & Flow
HEATH LEDGER—Brokeback Mountain
JOAQUIN PHOENIX—Walk the Line
DAVID STRATHAIRN—Good Night, and Good Luck

ACTRESS

★ **REESE WITHERSPOON—Walk the Line**
JUDI DENCH—Mrs. Henderson Presents
FELICITY HUFFMAN—Transamerica
KEIRA KNIGHTLEY—Pride & Prejudice
CHARLIZE THERON—North Country

SUPPORTING ACTOR

★ **GEORGE CLOONEY—Syriana**
MATT DILLON—Crash
PAUL GIAMATTI—Cinderella Man
JAKE GYLLENHAAL—Brokeback Mountain
WILLIAM HURT—A History of Violence

SUPPORTING ACTRESS

★ **RACHEL WEISZ—The Constant Gardener**
AMY ADAMS—Junebug
CATHERINE KEENER—Capote
FRANCES McDORMAND—North Country
MICHELLE WILLIAMS—Brokeback Mountain

DIRECTOR

★ **BROKEBACK MOUNTAIN—Ang Lee**
CAPOTE—Bennett Miller
CRASH—Paul Haggis
GOOD NIGHT, AND GOOD LUCK—George Clooney
MUNICH—Steven Spielberg

CINEMATOGPHAPHY

★ **MEMOIRS OF A GEISHA--Dion Beebe**
BATMAN BEGINS—Wally Pfister
BROKEBACK MOUNTAIN—Rodrigo Prieto
GOOD NIGHT, AND GOOD LUCK—Robert Elswit
THE NEW WORLD—Emmanuel Lubezki

SCORE

★ **BROKEBACK MOUNTAIN—Gustavo Santaolalla**
THE CONSTANT GARDENER—Alberto Iglesias
MEMOIRS OF A GEISHA—John Williams
MUNICH—John Williams
PRIDE & PREJUDICE—Dario Marianelli

SONG

★ **IT'S HARD OUT HERE FOR A PIMP*** *from* **Hustle & Flow**
IN THE DEEP *from* Crash
TRAVELIN' THRU *from* Transamerica

VISUAL EFFECTS

★ **KING KONG**
THE CHRONICLES OF NARNIA: THE LION, THE WITCH, AND THE WARDROBE
WAR OF THE WORLDS

ANIMATED FILM

★ **WALLACE & GROMIT: THE CURSE OF THE WERE-RABBIT**
HOWL'S MOVING CASTLE
TIM BURTON'S CORPSE BRIDE

2007

BEST PICTURE

★ **THE DEPARTED**
  BABEL
  LETTERS FROM IWO JIMA
  LITTLE MISS SUNSHINE
  THE QUEEN

ACTOR

★ **FOREST WHITAKER—The Last King of Scotland**
  LEONARDO DiCAPRIO—Blood Diamond*
  RYAN GOSLING—Half Nelson
  PETER O'TOOLE—Venus
  WILL SMITH—The Pursuit of Happyness

ACTRESS

★ **HELEN MIRREN—The Queen**
  PENÉLOPE CRUZ—Volver
  JUDI DENCH—Notes on a Scandal
  MERYL STREEP—The Devil Wears Prada
  KATE WINSLET—Little Children

SUPPORTING ACTOR

★ **ALAN ARKIN—Little Miss Sunshine**
  JACKIE EARLE HALEY—Little Children
  DJIMON HOUNSOU—Blood Diamond
  EDDIE MURPHY—Dreamgirls
  MARK WAHLBERG—The Departed

SUPPORTING ACTRESS

★ **JENNIFER HUDSON—Dreamgirls**
  ADRIANA BARRAZA—Babel
  CATE BLANCHETT—Notes on a Scandal
  ABIGAIL BRESLIN—Little Miss Sunshine
  RINKO KIKUCHI—Babel

DIRECTOR

★ **THE DEPARTED—Martin Scorsese**
BABEL—Alejandro González Iñárritu
LETTERS FROM IWO JIMA—Clint Eastwood
THE QUEEN—Stephen Frears
UNITED 93—Paul Greengrass

CINEMATOGPHAPHY

★ **PAN'S LABYRINTH—Guillermo Navarro**
THE BLACK DAHLIA—Vilmos Zsigmond
CHILDREN OF MEN—Emmanuel Lubezki
THE ILLUSIONIST—Dick Pope
THE PRESTIGE—Wally Pfister

SCORE

★ **BABEL—Gustavo Santaolalla**
THE GOOD GERMAN—Thomas Newman
NOTES ON A SCANDAL—Philip Glass
PAN'S LABYRINTH—Javier Navarrete
THE QUEEN—Alexandre Desplat

SONG

★ **I NEED TO WAKE UP** *from* **An Inconvenient Truth**
LISTEN *from* Dreamgirls
LOVE YOU I DO *from* Dreamgirls
OUR TOWN *from* Cars
PATIENCE *from* Dreamgirls

VISUAL EFFECTS

★ **PIRATES OF THE CARIBBEAN: DEAD MAN'S CHEST**
POSEIDON
SUPERMAN RETURNS

ANIMATED FILM

★ **HAPPY FEET**
CARS
MONSTER HOUSE

2008

*Doing a "De Niro," Swinton piles on pounds for winning role, trims down for Oscar night.

BEST PICTURE

★ **NO COUNTRY FOR OLD MEN**
ATONEMENT
JUNO
MICHAEL CLAYTON
THERE WILL BE BLOOD

ACTOR

★ **DANIEL DAY-LEWIS—There Will Be Blood**
GEORGE CLOONEY—Michael Clayton
JOHNNY DEPP—Sweeney Todd: The Demon Barber of Fleet Street
TOMMY LEE JONES—In the Valley of Elah
VIGGO MORTENSEN—Eastern Promises

ACTRESS

★ **MARION COTILLARD—La Vie en Rose**
CATE BLANCHETT—Elizabeth: The Golden Age
JULIE CHRISTIE—Away from Her
LAURA LINNEY—The Savages
ELLEN PAGE—Juno

SUPPORTING ACTOR

★ **JAVIER BARDEM—No Country for Old Men**
CASEY AFFLECK—The Assassination of Jesse James by the Coward Robert Ford
PHILIP SEYMOUR HOFFMAN—Charlie Wilson's War
HAL HOLBROOK—Into the Wild
TOM WILKINSON—Michael Clayton

SUPPORTING ACTRESS

★ **TILDA SWINTON—Michael Clayton***
CATE BLANCHETT—I'm Not There
RUBY DEE—American Gangster
SAOIRSE RONAN—Atonement
AMY RYAN—Gone Baby Gone

DIRECTOR

★ **NO COUNTRY FOR OLD MEN—Joel Coen and Ethan Coen**
THE DIVING BELL AND THE BUTTERFLY—Julian Schnabel
JUNO—Jason Reitman
MICHAEL CLAYTON—Tony Gilroy
THERE WILL BE BLOOD—Paul Thomas Anderson

CINEMATOGRAPHY

★ **THERE WILL BE BLOOD—Robert Elswit**
THE ASSASSINATION OF JESSE JAMES BY THE COWARD
ROBERT FORD—Roger Deakins
ATONEMENT—Seamus McGarvey
THE DIVING BELL AND THE BUTTERFLY—Janusz Kamiński
NO COUNTRY FOR OLD MEN—Roger Deakins

SCORE

★ **ATONEMENT—Dario Marianelli**
3:10 TO YUMA—Marco Baltrami
THE KITE RUNNER—Alberto Iglasias
MICHAEL CLAYTON—James Newton Howard
RATATOUILLE—Michael Giacchino

SONG

★ **FALLING SLOWLY** *from* **Once**
HAPPY WORKING SONG *from* Enchanted
RAISE IT UP *from* August Rush
SO CLOSE *from* Enchanted
THAT'S HOW YOU KNOW *from* Enchanted

VISUAL EFFECTS

★ **THE GOLDEN COMPASS**
PIRATES OF THE CARIBBEAN: AT WORLD'S END
TRANSFORMERS

ANIMATED FILM

★ **RATATOUILLE**
PERSEPOLIS
SURF'S UP

2009

Ledger posthumous win.

BEST PICTURE

★ **SLUMDOG MILLIONAIRE**
THE CURIOUS CASE OF BENJAMIN BUTTON
FROST/NIXON
MILK
THE READER

ACTOR

★ **SEAN PENN—Milk**
RICHARD JENKINS—The Visitor
FRANK LANGELLA—Frost/Nixon
BRAD PITT—The Curious Case of Benjamin Button
MICKEY ROURKE—The Wrestler

ACTRESS

★ **KATE WINSLET—The Reader**
ANNE HATHAWAY—Rachel Getting Married
ANGELINA JOLIE—Changeling
MELISSA LEO—Frozen River
MERYL STREEP—Doubt

SUPPORTING ACTOR

★ **HEATH LEDGER—The Dark Knight***
JOSH BROLIN—Milk
ROBERT DOWNEY JR.—Tropic Thunder
PHILIP SEYMOUR HOFFMAN—Doubt
MICHAEL SHANNON—Revolutionary Road

SUPPORTING ACTRESS

★ **PENÉLOPE CRUZ—Vicky Cristina Barcelona**
AMY ADAMS—Doubt
VIOLA DAVIS—Doubt
TARAJI P. HENSON—The Curious Case of Benjamin Button
MARISA TOMEI—The Wrestler

DIRECTOR

★ **SLUMDOG MILLIONAIRE—Danny Boyle**
THE CURIOUS CASE OF BENJAMIN BUTTON—David Fincher
FROST/NIXON—Ron Howard
MILK—Gus Van Sant
THE READER—Stephen Daldry

CINEMATOGRAPHY

★ **SLUMDOG MILLIONAIRE—Anthony Dod Mantle**
CHANGELING—Tom Stern
THE CURIOUS CASE OF BENJAMIN BUTTON—Claudio
    Miranda
THE DARK NIGHT—Wally Pfister
THE READER—Chris Menges and Roger Deakins

SCORE

★ **SLUMDOG MILLIONAIRE—A.R. Rahman**
THE CURIOUS CASE OF BENJAMIN BUTTON—Alexandre
    Desplat
DEFIANCE—James Newton Howard
MILK—Danny Elfman
WALL-E—Thomas Newman

SONG

★ **JAI HO** *from* **Slumdog Millionaire**
DOWN TO EARTH *from* WALL-E
O SAYA *from* Slumdog Millionaire

VISUAL EFFECTS

★ **THE CURIOUS CASE OF BENJAMIN BUTTON**
THE DARK KNIGHT
IRON MAN

ANIMATED FILM

★ **WALL-E**
BOLT
KUNG FU PANDA

2010

Rule change increases nominees for Best Picture to ten.

BEST PICTURE

★ **THE HURT LOCKER**   AVATAR
 THE BLIND SIDE   DISTRICT 9
 AN EDUCATION   INGLOURIOUS BASTERDS
 PRECIOUS   A SERIOUS MAN
 UP   UP IN THE AIR

ACTOR

★ **JEFF BRIDGES—Crazy Heart**
 GEORGE CLOONEY—Up in the Air
 COLIN FIRTH—A Single Man
 MORGAN FREEMAN—Invictus
 JEREMY RENNER—The Hurt Locker

ACTRESS

★ **SANDRA BULLOCK—The Blind Side**
 HELEN MIRREN—The Last Station
 CAREY MULLIGAN—An Education
 GABOUREY SIDIBE—Precious
 MERYL STREEP—Julie & Julia

SUPPORTING ACTOR

★ **CHRISTOPH WALTZ—Inglourious Basterds**
 MATT DAMON—Invictus
 WOODY HARRELSON—The Messenger
 CHRISTOPHER PLUMMER—The Last Station
 STANLEY TUCCI—The Lovely Bones

SUPPORTING ACTRESS

★ **MO'NIQUE—Precious**
 PENÉLOPE CRUZ—Nine
 VERA FARMIGA—Up in the Air
 MAGGIE GYLLENHAAL—Crazy Heart
 ANNA KENDRICK—Up in the Air

DIRECTOR

★ **THE HURT LOCKER—Kathryn Bigelow**
AVATAR—James Cameron
INGLOURIOUS BASTERDS—Quentin Tarantino
PRECIOUS—Lee Daniels
UP IN THE AIR—Jason Reitman

CINEMATOGRAPHY

★ **AVATAR—Mauro Fiore**
HARRY POTTER AND THE HALF-BLOOD PRINCE—Bruno
   Delbonnel
THE HURT LOCKER—Barry Ackroyd
INGLOURIOUS BASTERDS—Robert Richardson
THE WHITE RIBBON—Christian Berger

SCORE

★ **UP—Michael Giacchino**
AVATAR—James Horner
FANTASTIC MR. FOX—Alexandre Desplat
THE HURT LOCKER—Marco Beltrami and Buck Sanders
SHERLOCK HOLMES—Hans Zimmer

SONG

★ **THE WEARY KIND** *from* **Crazy Heart**
ALMOST THERE *from* The Princess and the Frog
DOWN IN NEW ORLEANS *from* The Princess and the Frog
LOIN DE PANAME *from* Paris 36
TAKE IT ALL *from* NINE

VISUAL EFFECTS

★ **AVATAR**
DISTRICT 9
STAR TREK

ANIMATED FILM

★ **UP**
CORALINE
FANTASTIC MR. FOX
THE PRINCESS AND THE FROG
THE SECRET OF KELLS

2011

BEST PICTURE

★ **THE KING'S SPEECH**
  BLACK SWAN
  INCEPTION
  THE SOCIAL NETWORK
  TRUE GRIT

  127 HOURS
  THE FIGHTER
  THE KIDS ARE ALL RIGHT
  TOY STORY 3
  WINTER'S BONE

ACTOR

★ **COLIN FIRTH—The King's Speech**
  JAVIER BARDEM—Biutiful
  JEFF BRIDGES—True Grit
  JESSE EISENBERG—The Social Network
  JAMES FRANCO—127 Hours

ACTRESS

★ **NATALIE PORTMAN—Black Swan**
  ANNETTE BENING—The Kids Are All Right
  NICOLE KIDMAN—Rabbit Hole
  JENNIFER LAWRENCE—Winter's Bone
  MICHELLE WILLIAMS—Blue Valentine

SUPPORTING ACTOR

★ **CHRISTIAN BALE—The Fighter**
  JOHN HAWKES—Winter's Bone
  JEREMY RENNER—The Town
  MARK RUFFALO—The Kids Are All Right
  GEOFFREY RUSH—The King's Speech

SUPPORTING ACTRESS

★ **MELISSA LEO—The Fighter**
  AMY ADAMS—The Fighter
  HELENA BONHAM CARTER—The King's Speech
  HAILEE STEINFELD—True Grit
  JACKI WEAVER—Animal Kingdom

DIRECTOR

★ **THE KING'S SPEECH—Tom Hooper**
BLACK SWAN—Darren Aronofsky
THE FIGHTER—David O. Russell
THE SOCIAL NETWORK—David Fincher
TRUE GRIT—Joel Coen and Ethan Coen

CINEMATOGRAPHY

★ **INCEPTION—Wally Pfister**
BLACK SWAN—Matthew Libatique
THE KING'S SPEECH—Danny Cohen
THE SOCIAL NETWORK—Jeff Cronenweth
TRUE GRIT—Roger Deakins

SCORE

★ **THE SOCIAL NETWORK—Trent Reznor and Atticus Ross**
127 HOURS—A.R. Rahman
HOW TO TRAIN YOUR DRAGON—John Powell
INCEPTION—Hans Zimmer
THE KING'S SPEECH—Alexandre Desplat

SONG

★ **WE BELONG TOGETHER** *from* **Toy Story 3**
COMING HOME *from* Country Strong
I SEE THE LIGHT *from* Tangled
IF I RISE *from* 127 Hours

VISUAL EFFECTS

★ **INCEPTION**
ALICE IN WONDERLAND
HARRY POTTER AND THE DEATHLY HALLOWS
HEREAFTER
IRON MAN 2

ANIMATED FILM

★ **TOY STORY 3**
HOW TO TRAIN YOUR DRAGON
THE ILLUSIONIST

2012

*Celebrating 50 years of James Bond films,
at 75, Shirley Bassey sings* GOLDFINGER.

BEST PICTURE

★ **THE ARTIST**   THE DESCENDANTS
   THE HELP   HUGO
   MIDNIGHT IN PARIS   MONEYBALL
   THE TREE OF LIFE   WAR HORSE
   EXTREMELY LOUD
      & INCREDIBLY CLOSE

ACTOR

★ **JEAN DUJARDIN—The Artist**
   DEMIÁN BICHIR—A Better Life
   GEORGE CLOONEY—The Descendants
   GARY OLDMAN—Tinker Tailor Soldier Spy
   BRAD PITT—Moneyball

ACTRESS

★ **MERYL STREEP—The Iron Lady**
   GLENN CLOSE—Albert Nobbs
   VIOLA DAVIS—The Help
   ROONEY MARA—The Girl With the Dragon Tattoo
   MICHELLE WILLIAMS—My Week With Marilyn

SUPPORTING ACTOR

★ **CHRISTOPHER PLUMMER—Beginners**
   KENNETH BRANAGH—My Week with Marilyn
   JONAH HILL—Moneyball
   NICK NOLTE—Warrior
   MAX VON SYDOW—Extremely Loud & Incredibly Close

SUPPORTING ACTRESS

★ **OCTAVIA SPENCER—The Help**
   BÉRÉNICE BEJO—The Artist
   JESSICA CHASTAIN—The Help
   MELISSA McCARTHY—Bridesmaids
   JANET McTEER—Albert Nobbs

84th ACADEMY AWARDS   Hosted by Billy Crystal

DIRECTOR

★ **THE ARTIST—Michel Hazanavicius**
THE DESCENDANTS—Alexander Payne
HUGO—Martin Scorsese
MIDNIGHT IN PARIS—Woody Allen
THE TREE OF LIFE—Terrence Malick

CINEMATOGRAPHY

★ **HUGO—Robert Richardson**
THE ARTIST—Guillaume Schiffman
THE GIRL WITH THE DRAGON TATTOO—Jeff Cronenweth
THE TREE OF LIFE—Emmanuel Lubezki
WAR HORSE—Janusz Kamiński

SCORE

★ **THE ARTIST—Ludovic Bource**
THE ADVENTURES OF TINTIN: THE SECRET OF
   THE UNICORN—John Williams
HUGO—Howard Shore
TINKER TAILOR SOLDIER SPY—Alberto Iglesias
WAR HORSE—John Williams

SONG

★ **MAN OR MUPPET** *from* **The Muppets**
REAL IN RIO *from* Rio

VISUAL EFFECTS

★ **HUGO**
HARRY POTTER AND THE DEATHLY HALLOWS
REAL STEEL
RISE OF THE PLANET OF THE APES
TRANSFORMERS: DARK OF THE MOON

ANIMATED FILM

★ **RANGO**
A CAT IN PARIS
CHICO AND RITA
KUNG FU PANDA 2
PUSS IN BOOTS

2013

*Phoenix's PETA ad of dying fish too provocative for Oscars;
ABC moves it to after-show.*

BEST PICTURE

★ **ARGO**
DJANGO UNCHAINED
LIFE OF PI
SILVER LININGS PLAYBOOK
BEASTS OF THE SOUTHERN
   WILD
AMOUR
LES MISÉRABLES
LINCOLN
ZERO DARK THIRTY

ACTOR

★ **DANIEL DAY-LEWIS—Lincoln**
BRADLEY COOPER—Silver Linings Playbook
HUGH JACKMAN—Les Misérables
JOAQUIN PHOENIX—The Master*
DENZEL WASHINGTON—Flight

ACTRESS

★ **JENNIFER LAWRENCE—Silver Linings Playbook**
JESSICA CHASTAIN—Zero Dark Thirty
EMMANUELLE RIVA—Amour
QUVENZHANÉ WALLIS—Beasts of the Southern Wild
NAOMI WATTS—The Impossible

SUPPORTING ACTOR

★ **CHRISTOPH WALTZ—Django Unchained**
ALAN ARKIN—Argo
ROBERT DE NIRO—Silver Linings Playbook
PHILIP SEYMOUR HOFFMAN—The Master
TOMMY LEE JONES—Lincoln

SUPPORTING ACTRESS

★ **ANNE HATHAWAY—Les Misérables**
AMY ADAMS—The Master
SALLY FIELD—Lincoln
HELEN HUNT—The Sessions
JACKI WEAVER—Silver Linings Playbook

DIRECTOR

★ **LIFE OF PI—Ang Lee**
AMOUR—Michael Haneke
BEASTS OF THE SOUTHERN WILD—Benh Zeitlin
LINCOLN—Steven Spielberg
SILVER LININGS PLAYBOOK—David O. Russell

CINEMATOGRAPHY

★ **LIFE OF PI—Claudio Miranda**
ANNA KARENINA—Seamus McGarvey
DJANGO UNCHAINED—Robert Richardson
LINCOLN—Janusz Kamiński
SKYFALL—Roger Deakins

SCORE

★ **LIFE OF PI—Mychael Danna**
ANNA KARENINA—Dario Marianelli
ARGO—Alexandre Despiat
LINCOLN—John Williams
SKYFALL—Thomas Newman

SONG

★ **SKYFALL** *from* **Skyfall**
BEFORE MY TIME *from* Chasing Ice
EVERYBODY NEEDS A BEST FRIEND *from* Ted
PI'S LULLABY *from* Life if Pi
SUDDENLY from Les Misérables

VISUAL EFFECTS

★ **LIFE OF PI**
THE AVENGERS
THE HOBBIT: AN UNEXPECTED JOURNEY
PROMETHEUS
SNOW WHITE AND THE HUNTSMAN

ANIMATED FILM

★ **BRAVE**
FRANKENWEENIE
PARANORMAN
THE PIRATES! BAND OF MISFITS
WRECK-IT RALPH

Dolby Theater, Hollywood   February 24, 2013

2014

Streep brings record-breakin acting nominations to 18.
With GREAT BEAUTY, *Italy tops 57 countries with 14 Foreign Film wins.*

BEST PICTURE

★ **12 YEARS A SLAVE**   AMERICAN HUSTLE
  CAPTAIN PHILLIPS   DALLAS BUYERS CLUB
  GRAVITY   HER
  NEBRASKA   PHILOMENA
  THE WOLF OF WALL STREET

ACTOR

★ **MATTHEW McCONAUGHEY—Dallas Buyers Club**
  CHRISTIAN BALE—American Hustle
  BRUCE DERN—Nebraska
  LEONARDO DiCAPRIO—The Wolf of Wall Street
  CHIWETEL EJIOFOR—12 Years a Slave

ACTRESS

★ **CATE BLANCHETT—Blue Jasmine**
  AMY ADAMS—American Hustle
  SANDRA BULLOCK—Gravity
  JUDI DENCH—Philomena
  MERYL STREEP—August: Osage County*

SUPPORTING ACTOR

★ **JARED LETO—Dallas Buyers Club**
  BARKHAD ABDI—Captain Phillips
  BRADLEY COOPER—American Hustle
  MICHAEL FASSBENDER—12 Years a Slave
  JONAH HILL—The Wolf of Wall Street

SUPPORTING ACTRESS

★ **LUPITA NYONG'O—12 Years a Slave**
  SALLEY HAWKINS—Blue Jasmine
  JENNIFER LAWRENCE—American Hustle
  JULIA ROBERTS—August: Osage County
  JUNE SQUIBB—Nebraska

DIRECTOR

★ **GRAVITY—Alfonso Cuarón**
12 YEARS A SLAVE—Steve McQueen
AMERICAN HUSTLE—David O. Russell
NEBRASKA—Alexander Payne
THE WOLF OF WALL STREET—Martin Scorsese

CINEMATOGRAPHY

★ **GRAVITY—Emmanuel Lubezki**
THE GRANDMASTER—Philippe Le Sourd
INSIDE LLEWYN DAVIS—Bruno Delbonnel
NEBRASKA—Phedon Papamichael
PRISONERS—Roger Deakins

SCORE

★ **GRAVITY—Steven Price**
THE BOOK THIEF—John Williams
HER—William Butler and Owen Pallett
PHILOMENA—Alexandre Desplat
SAVING MR. BANKS—Thomas Newman

SONG

★ **LET IT GO** *from* **Frozen**
HAPPY *from* Despicable Me 2
THE MOON SONG *from* Her
ORDINARY LOVE *from* Mandela: Long Walk to Freedom

VISUAL EFFECTS

★ **GRAVITY**
THE HOBBIT: THE DESOLATION OF SMAUG
IRON MAN 3
THE LONE RANGER
STAR TREK INTO DARKNESS

ANIMATED FILM

★ **FROZEN**
THE CROODS
DISPICABLE ME 2
ERNEST & CELESTINE
THE WIND RISES

2015

Julie Andrews embraces Lady Gaga onstage after
SOUND OF MUSIC *50th Anniversary musical tribute.*

BEST PICTURE

★ **BIRDMAN or (The Unexpected Virtue of Ignorance)**
AMERICAN SNIPER   BOYHOOD
THE GRAND BUDAPEST HOTEL   THE IMITATION GAME
SELMA   WHIPLASH
THE THEORY OF EVERYTHING

ACTOR

★ **EDDIE REDMAYNE—The Theory of Everything**
STEVE CARELL—Foxcatcher
BRADLEY COOPER—American Sniper
BENEDICT CUMBERBATCH—The Imitation Game
MICHAEL KEATON—Birdman ...

ACTRESS

★ **JULIANNE MOORE—Still Alice**
MARION COTILLARD—Two Days, One Night
FELICITY JONES—The Theory of Everything
ROSAMUND PIKE—Gone Girl
REESE WITHERSPOON—Wild

SUPPORTING ACTOR

★ **J.K. SIMMONS—Whiplash**
ROBERT DUVALL—The Judge
ETHAN HAWKE—Boyhood
EDWARD NORTON—Birdman ...
MARK RUFFALO—Foxcatcher

SUPPORTING ACTRESS

★ **PATRICIA ARQUETTE—Boyhood**
LAURA DERN—Wild
KEIRA KNIGHTLEY—The Imitation Game
EMMA STONE—Birdman ...
MERYL STREEP—Into the Woods

DIRECTOR

★ **BIRDMAN—Alejandro G. Iñárritu**
BOYHOOD—Richard Linklater
FOXCATCHER—Bennett Miller
THE GRAND BUDAPEST HOTEL—Wes Anderson
THE IMITATION GAME—Morten Tyldum

CINEMATOGRAPHY

★ **BIRDMAN—Emmanuel Lubezki**
THE GRAND BUDAPEST HOTEL—Robert Yeoman
IDA—Łukasz Żal and Ryszard Lenczewski
MR. TURNER—Dick Pope
UNBROKEN—Roger Deakins

SCORE

★ **THE GRAND BUDAPEST HOTEL—Alexandre Desplat**
THE IMITATION GAME—Alexandre Desplat
INTERSTELLAR—Hans Zimmer
MR. TURNER—Gary Yershon
THE THEORY OF EVERYTHING—Jóhann Jóhannsson

SONG

★ **GLORY** *from* **Selma**
EVERYTHING IS AWESOME *from* The Lego Movie
GRATEFUL *from* Beyond the Lights
I'M NOT GONNA MISS YOU *from* Glen Campbell...I'll Be Me
LOST STARS *from* Begin Again

VISUAL EFFECTS

★ **INTERSTELLER**
CAPTAIN AMERICA: THE WINTER SOLDIER
DAWN OF THE PLANET OF THE APES
GUARDIANS OF THE GALAXY
X-MEN: DAYS OF FUTURE PAST

ANIMATED FILM

★ **BIG HERO 6**
THE BOXTROLLS
HOW TO TRAIN YOUR DRAGON 2
SONG OF THE SEA
THE TALE OF THE PRINCESS KAGUYA

2016

Increasing protests over lack of diversity in nominations.
Chris Rock posts Oscar promo on Twitter: "The White BET Awards."

BEST PICTURE

★ **SPOTLIGHT**
BRIDGE OF SPIES
MAD MAX: FURY ROAD
THE REVENANT
THE BIG SHORT
BROOKLYN
THE MARTIAN
ROOM

ACTOR

★ **LEONARDO DiCAPRIO—The Revenant**
BRYAN CRANSTON—Trumbo
MATT DAMON—The Martian
MICHAEL FASSBENDER—Steve Jobs
EDDIE REDMAYNE—The Danish Girl

ACTRESS

★ **BRIE LARSON—Room**
CATE BLANCHETT—Carol
JENNIFER LAWRENCE—Joy
CHARLOTTE RAMPLING—45 Years
SAOIRSE RONAN—Brooklyn

SUPPORTING ACTOR

★ **MARK RYLANCE—Bridge of Spies**
CHRISTIAN BALE—The Big Short
TOM HARDY—The Revenant
MARK RUFFALO—Spotlight
SYLVESTER STALLONE—Creed

SUPPORTING ACTRESS

★ **ALICIA VIKANDER—The Danish Girl**
JENNIFER JASON LEIGH—The Hateful Eight
ROONEY MARA—Carol
RACHEL McADAMS—Spotlight
KATE WINSLET—Steve Jobs

DIRECTOR

★ **THE REVENANT—Alejandro G. Iñárritu**
THE BIG SHORT—Adam McKay
MAD MAX: FURY ROAD—George Miller
ROOM—Lenny Abrahamson
SPOTLIGHT—Tom McCarthy

CINEMATOGRAPHY

★ **THE REVENANT—Emmanuel Lubezki**
CAROL—Edward Lachman
THE HATEFUL EIGHT—Robert Richardson
MAD MAX: FURY ROAD—John Seale
SICARIO—Roger Deakins

SCORE

★ **THE HATEFUL EIGHT—Ennio Morricone**
BRIDGE OF SPIES—Thomas Newman
CAROL—Carter Burwell
SICARIO—Jóhann Jóhannsson
STAR WARS: THE FORCE AWAKENS—John Williams

SONG

★ **WRITING'S ON THE WALL** *from* **Spectre**
EARNED IT *from* Fifty Shades of Grey
MANTA RAY *from* Racing Extinction
SIMPLE SONG #3 *from* Youth
TIL IT HAPPENS TO YOU *from* The Hunting Ground

VISUAL EFFECTS

★ **EX MACHINA**
MAD MAX: FURY ROAD
THE MARTIAN
THE REVENANT
STAR WARS: THE FORCE AWAKENS

ANIMATED FILM

★ **INSIDE OUT**
ANOMALISA
BOY AND THE WORLD
SHAUN THE SHEEP MOVIE
WHEN MARNIE WAS THERE

2017

*LA LA LAND *producers run to accept Best Picture Oscar,
only to learn wrong envelope was read.*

BEST PICTURE

★ **MOONLIGHT***　　　　ARRIVAL
　FENCES　　　　　　　　HACKSAW RIDGE
　HELL OR HIGH WATER　　HIDDEN FIGURES
　LA LA LAND*　　　　　　LION
　MANCHESTER BY THE SEA

ACTOR

★ **CASEY AFFLECK—Manchester by the Sea**
　ANDREW GARFIELD—Hacksaw Ridge
　RYAN GOSLING—La La Land
　VIGGO MORTENSEN—Captain Fantastic
　DENZEL WASHINGTON—Fences

ACTRESS

★ **EMMA STONE—La La Land**
　ISABELLE HUPPERT—Elle
　RUTH NEGGA—Loving
　NATALIE PORTMAN—Jackie
　MERYL STREEP—Florence Foster Jenkins

SUPPORTING ACTOR

★ **MAHERSHALA ALI—Moonlight**
　JEFF BRIDGES—Hell or High Water
　LUCAS HEDGES—Manchester by the Sea
　DEV PATEL—Lion
　MICHAEL SHANNON—Nocturnal Animals

SUPPORTING ACTRESS

★ **VIOLA DAVIS—Fences**
　NAOMIE HARRIS—Moonlight
　NICOLE KIDMAN—Lion
　OCTAVIA SPENCER—Hidden Figures
　MICHELLE WILLIAMS—Manchester by the Sea

DIRECTOR

★ **LA LA LAND—Damien Chazelle**
ARRIVAL—Denis Villeneuve
HACKSAW RIDGE—Mel Gibson
MANCHESTER BY THE SEA—Kenneth Lonergan
MOONLIGHT—Barry Jenkins

CINEMATOGRAPHY

★ **LA LA LAND—Linus Sandgren**
ARRIVAL—Bradford Young
LION—Greig Fraser
MOONLIGHT—James Laxton
SILENCE—Rodrigo Prieto

SCORE

★ **LA LA LAND—Justin Hurwitz**
JACKIE—Mica Levi
LION—Dustin O'Halloran and Hauschka
MOONLIGHT—Nicholas Britell
PASSENGERS—Thomas Newman

SONG

★ **CITY OF STARS** *from* **La La Land**
AUDITION (The Fools Who Dream) *from* La La Land
CAN'T STOP THE FEELING *from* Trolls
THE EMPTY CHAIR *from* Jim: The James Foley Story
HOW FAR I'LL GO *from* Moana

VISUAL EFFECTS

★ **THE JUNGLE BOOK**
DEEPWATER HORIZON
DOCTOR STRANGE
KUBO AND THE TWO STRINGS
ROGUE ONE: A STAR WARS STORY

ANIMATED FILM

★ **ZOOTOPIA**
KUBO AND THE TWO STRINGS
MOANA
MY LIFE AS A ZUCCHINI
THE RED TURTLE

2018

New "Most Popular Film" category: in;
New "Most Popular Film" category: out.

BEST PICTURE

★ **THE SHAPE OF WATER**
  DARKEST HOUR
  GET OUT
  PHANTOM THREAD
  THREE BILLBOARDS OUTSIDE
    EBBING, MISSOURI
  CALL ME BY YOUR NAME
  DUNKIRK
  LADY BIRD
  THE POST

ACTOR

★ **GARY OLDMAN—Darkest Hour**
  TIMOTHÉE CHALAMET—Call Me by Your Name
  DANIEL DAY-LEWIS—Phantom Thread
  DANIEL KALUUYA—Get Out
  DENZEL WASHINGTON—Roman J. Israel, Esq.

ACTRESS

★ **FRANCES McDORMAND—Three Billboards**
  Outside Ebbing, Missouri
  SALLY HAWKINS—The Shape of Water
  MARGOT ROBBIE—I, Tonya
  SAOIRES RONAN—Lady Bird
  MERYL STREEP—The Post

SUPPORTING ACTOR

★ **SAM ROCKWELL—Three Billboards Outside Ebbing,**
  Missouri
  WILLEM DAFOE—The Florida Project
  WOODY HARRELSON—Three Billboards Outside Ebbing,
    Missouri
  RICHARD JENKINS—The Shape of Water
  CHRISTOPHER PLUMMER—All the Money in the World

SUPPORTING ACTRESS

★ **ALLISON JANNEY—I, Tonya**
  MARY J. BLIGE—Mudbound
  LESLEY MANVILLE—Phantom Thread
  LAURIE METCALF—Lady Bird
  OCTAVIA SPENCER—The Shape of Water

DIRECTOR

★ **THE SHAPE OF WATER—Guillermo del Toro**
DUNKIRK—Christopher Nolan
GET OUT—Jordan Peele
LADY BIRD—Greta Gerwig
PHANTOM THREAD—Paul Thomas Anderson

CINEMATOGRAPHY

★ **BLADE RUNNER 2049—Roger Deakins**
DARKEST HOUR—Bruno Delbonnel
DUNKIRK—Hoyte van Hoytema
MUDBOUND—Rachel Morrison
THE SHAPE OF WATER—Dan Lausten

SCORE

★ **THE SHAPE OF WATER—Alexandre Desplat**
DUNKIRK—Hans Zimmer
PHANTOM THREAD—Jonny Greenwood
STAR WARS: THE LAST JEDI—John Williams
THREE BILLBOARDS OUTSIDE EBBING, MISSOURI
—Carter Burwell

SONG

★ **REMEMBER ME** *from* **Coco**
MIGHTY RIVER *from* Mudbound
MYSTERY OF LOVE *from* Call Me by Your Name
STAND UP FOR SOMETHING *from* Marshall
THIS IS ME *from* The Greatest Showman

VISUAL EFFECTS

★ **BLADE RUNNER 2049**
GUARDIANS OF THE GALAXY VOL. 2
KONG: SKULL ISLAND
STAR WARS: THE LAST JEDI
WAR FOR THE PLANET OF THE APES

ANIMATED FILM

★ **COCO**
THE BOSS BABY
THE BREADWINNER
FERDINAND
LOVING VINCENT

2019

Host Kevin Hart in;
Host Kevin Hart (and gay jokes) out.

BEST PICTURE

★ **GREEN BOOK**   BLACK PANTHER
  BLACKkKLANSMAN   BOHEMIAN RHAPSODY
  THE FAVOURITE   ROMA
  A STAR IS BORN   VICE

ACTOR

★ **RAMI MALEK—Bohemian Rhapsody**
  CHRISTIAN BALE—Vice
  BRADLEY COOPER—A Star Is Born
  WILLEM DAFOE—At Eternity's Gate
  VIGGO MORTENSEN—Green Book

ACTRESS

★ **OLIVIA COLMAN—The Favourite**
  YALITZA APARICIO—Roma
  GLENN CLOSE—The Wife
  LADY GAGA—A Star Is Born
  MELISSA McCARTHY—Can You Ever Forgive Me?

SUPPORTING ACTOR

★ **MAHERSHALA ALI—Green Book**
  ADAM DRIVER—BlacKkKlansman
  SAM ELLIOTT—A Star Is Born
  RICHARD E. GRANT—Can You Ever Forgive Me?
  SAM ROCKWELL—Vice

SUPPORTING ACTRESS

★ **REGINA KING—If Beale Street Could Talk**
  AMY ADAMS—Vice
  MARINA DE TAVIRA—Roma
  EMMA STONE—The Favourite
  RACHEL WEISZ—The Favourite

DIRECTOR

★ **ROMA—Alfonso Cuarón**
BLACKkKLANSMAN—Spike Lee
COLD WAR—Pawel Pawlikowski
THE FAVOURITE—Yorgos Lanthimos
VICE—Adam McKay

CINEMATOGRAPHY

★ **ROMA—Alfonso Cuarón**
COLD WAR—Łukasz Żal
THE FAVOURITE—Robbie Ryan
NEVER LOOK AWAY—Caleb Deschanel
A STAR IS BORN—Matthew Libatique

SCORE

★ **BLACK PANTHER—Ludwig Göransson**
BLACKkKLANSMAN—Terence Blanchard
IF BEALE STREET COULD TALK—Nicholas Britell
ISLE OF DOGS—Alexandre Desplat
MARY POPPINS RETURNS—Mark Shaiman

SONG

★ **SHALLOW *from* A Star is Born**
ALL THE STARS *from* Black Panther
I'LL FIGHT *from* RBG
THE PLACE WHERE LOST THINGS GO *from* Mary Poppins
Returns
WHEN A COWBOY TRADES HIS SPURS FOR WINGS *from*
The Ballad of Buster Scruggs

ORIGINAL SCREENPLAY

★ **GREEN BOOK**
THE FAVOURITE
FIRST REFORMED
ROMA
VICE

ADAPTED SCREENPLAY

★ **BLACKkKLANSMAN**
THE BALLAD OF BUSTER SCRUGGS
CAN YOU EVER FORGIVE ME
IF BEALE STREET COULD TALK
A STAR IS BORN

VISUAL EFFECTS

★ **FIRST MAN**
AVENGERS: INFINITY WAR
CHRISTOPHER ROBIN
READY PLAYER ONE
SOLO: A STAR WARS STORY

ANIMATED FILM

★ **SPIDER-MAN: INTO THE
SPIDER-VERSE**
INCREDIBLES 2
ISLE OF DOGS
MIRAI
RALPH BREAKS THE INTERNET

2020

Temporary rule permits non-theatrically released films.
Neilson rates tonight's TV viewership lowest ever.

BEST PICTURE

★ **PARASITE**
   FORD v FERRARI
   JOJO RABBIT
   LITTLE WOMEN
   ONCE UPON A TIME
     ...IN HOLLYWOOD

1917
THE IRISHMAN
JOKER
MARRIAGE STORY

ACTOR

★ **JOAQUIN PHOENIX—Joker**
   ANTONIO BANDERAS—Pain and Glory
   LEONARDO DiCAPRIO—Once Upon a Time
     ...in Hollywood
   ADAM DRIVER—Marriage Story
   JONATHAN PRYCE—The Two Popes

ACTRESS

★ **RENÉE ZELLWEGER—Judy**
   CYNTHIA ERIVO—Harriet
   SCARLETT JOHANSSON—Marriage Story
   SAOIRSE RONAN—Little Women
   CHARLIZE THERON—Bombshell

SUPPORTING ACTOR

★ **BRAD PITT—Once Upon a Time ...in Hollywood**
   TOM HANKS—A Beautiful Day in the Neighborhood
   ANTHONY HOPKINS—The Two Popes
   AL PACINO—The Irishman
   JOE PESCI—The Irishman

SUPPORTING ACTRESS

★ **LAURA DERN—Marriage Story**
   KATHY BATES—Richard Jewell
   SCARLETT JOHANSSON—Jojo Rabbit
   FLORENCE PUGH—Little Women
   MARGOT ROBBIE—Bombshell

DIRECTOR

★ **PARASITE—Bong Joon-ho**
1917—Sam Mendes
THE IRISHMAN—Martin Scorsese
JOKER—Todd Phillips
ONCE UPON A TIME ...IN HOLLYWOOD—Quentin Tarantino

CINEMATOGRAPHY

★ **1917—Roger Deakins**
THE IRISHMAN—Rodrigo Prieto
JOKER—Lawrence Sher
THE LIGHTHOUSE—Jarin Blaschke
ONCE UPON A TIME ...IN HOLLYWOOD—Robert Richardson

SCORE

★ **JOKER—Hildur Guðnadóttir**
1917—Thomas Newman
LITTLE WOMEN—Alexandre Desplat
MARRIAGE STORY—Randy Newman
STAR WARS: THE RISE OF SKYWALKER—John Williams

SONG

★ **(I'm Gonna) LOVE ME AGAIN** *from* **Rocketman**
I CANT LET YOU THROW YOURSELF AWAY *from* Toy Story 4
I'M STANDING WITH YOU *from* Breakthrough
INTO THE UNKNOWN *from* Frozen II
STAND UP *from* Harriet

ORIGINAL SCREENPLAY

★ **PARASITE**
1917
KNIVES OUT
MARRIAGE STORY
ONCE UPON A TIME IN
HOLLYWOOD

ADAPTED SCREENPLAY

★ **JOJO RABBIT**
THE IRISHMAN
JOKER
LITTLE WOMEN
THE TWO POPES

VISUAL EFFECTS

★ **1917**
AVENGERS: ENDGAME
THE IRISHMAN
THE LION KING
STAR WARS: THE RISE OF
SKYWALKER

ANIMATED FILM

★ **TOY STORY 4**
HOW TO TRAIN YOUR DRAGON:
THE HIDDEN WORLD
I LOST MY BODY
KLAUS
MISSING LINK

2021

Lamp-lit tables replace theater seating in year of pandemic.

Diversity quotas required for 2022 nominations.

BEST PICTURE

★ **NOMADLAND**
THE FATHER
JUDAS AND THE BLACK MESSIAH
MANK
MINARI
PROMISING YOUNG WOMAN
SOUND OF METAL
THE TRIAL OF THE CHICAGO 7

ACTOR

★ **ANTHONY HOPKINS—The Father**
RIZ AHMED—Sound of Metal
CHADWICK BOSEMAN—Ma Rainey's Black Bottom
GARY OLDMAN—Mank
STEVEN YEUN—Minari

ACTRESS

★ **FRANCES McDORMAND—Nomadland**
VIOLA DAVIS—Ma Rainey's Black Bottom
ANDRA DAY—The United States vs. Billy Holiday
VANESSA KIRBY—Pieces of a Woman
CAREY MULLIGAN—Promising Young Woman

SUPPORTING ACTOR

★ **DANIEL KALUUYA—Judas and the Black Messiah**
SACHA BARON COHEN—The Trial of the Chicago 7
LESLIE ODOM, JR—One Night in Miami...
PAUL RACI—Sound of Metal
LAKEITH STANFIELD—Judas and the Black Messiah

SUPPORTING ACTRESS

★ **YOUN YUH-JUNG—Minari**
MARIA BAKALOVA—Borat... Kazakhstan
GLENN CLOSE—Hillbilly Elegy
OLIVIA COLEMAN—The Father
AMANDA SEYFRIED—Mank

DIRECTOR

★ **NOMADLAND—Chloé Zhao**
ANOTHER ROUND—Thomas Vinterberg
MANK—David Fincher
MINARI—Lee Isaac Chung
PROMISING YOUNG WOMAN—Emerald Fennell

CINEMATOGRAPHY

★ **MANK—Eric Messerschmidt**
JUDAS AND THE BLACK MESSIAH—Sean Bobbitt
NEWS OF THE WORLD—Dariusz Wolski
NOMADLAND—Joshua James Richards
THE TRIAL OF THE CHICAGO 7—Phedon Papamichael

SCORE

★ **SOUL—Trent Reznor, Atticus Ross, Jon Batiste**
DA 5 BLOODS—Terence Blanchard
MANK—Trent Reznor and Atticus Ross
MINARI—Emile Mosseri
NEWS OF THE WORLD—James Newton Howard

SONG

★ **FIGHT FOR YOU** *from* **Judas and the Black Messiah**
HEAR MY VOICE *from* The Trial of the Chicago 7
HUSAVIK *from* Eurovision Song Contest: The Story of
Fire Saga
IO SÌ (Seen) *from* The Life Ahead (La Vita Davanti a Se)
SPEAK NOW *from* One Night in Miami...

ORIGINAL SCREENPLAY

★ **PROMISING YOUNG WOMAN**
JUDAS AND THE BLACK MESSIAH
MINARI
SOUND OF METAL
THE TRIAL OF THE CHICAGO 7

ADAPTED SCREENPLAY

★ **THE FATHER**
BORAT... KAZAKHSTAN
NOMADLAND
ONE NIGHT IN MIAMI...
THE WHITE TIGER

VISUAL EFFECTS

★ **TENET**
LOVE AND MONSTERS
THE MIDNIGHT SKY
MULAN
THE ONE AND ONLY IVAN

ANIMATED FILM

★ **SOUL**
ONWARD
OVER THE MOON
A SHAUN THE SHEEP
MOVIE: FARMAGEDDON
WOLFWALKERS

Union Station, Los Angeles   April 25, 2021

2022

Smith makes tearful, apologetic speech after bitch-slapping Chris Rock.

BEST PICTURE

★ **CODA**
DON'T LOOK UP
DUNE
LICORICE PIZZA
THE POWER OF THE DOG

BELFAST
DRIVE MY CAR
KING RICHARD
NIGHTMARE ALLEY
WEST SIDE STORY

ACTOR

★ **WILL SMITH—King Richard***
JAVIE BARDEM—Being the Ricardos
BENEDICT CUMBERBATCH—The Power of the Dog
ANDREW GARFIELD—tick, tick...BOOM!
DENZEL WASHINGTON—The Tragedy of Macbeth

ACTRESS

★ **JESSICA CHASTAIN—The Eyes of Tammy Fay**
OLIVIA COLMAN—The Lost Daughter
PENÉLOPE CRUZ—Parallel Mothers
NICOLE KIDMAN—Being the Ricardos
KRISTEN STEWART—Spencer

SUPPORTING ACTOR

★ **TROY KOTSUR—CODA**
CIARÁN HINDS—Belfast
JESSE PLEMONS—The Power of the Dog
J.K. SIMMONS—Being the Ricardos
KODI SMIT-McPHEE—The Power of the Dog

SUPPORTING ACTRESS

★ **ARIANA DeBOSE—West Side Story**
JESSIE BUCKLEY—The Lost Daughter
JUDI DENCH—Belfast
KIRSTEN DUNST—The Power of the Dog
AUNJANUE ELLIS—King Richard

DIRECTOR

★ **THE POWER OF THE DOG—Jane Campion**
BELFAST—Kenneth Branagh
DRIVE MY CAR—Ryusuke Hamaguchi
LICORICE PIZZA—Paul Thomas Anderson
WEST SIDE STORY—Stephen Spielberg

CINEMATOGRAPHY

★ **DUNE—Greig Fraser**
NIGHTMARE ALLEY—Dan Lausten
THE POWER OF THE DOG—Ari Wegner
THE TRAGEDY OF MACBETH—Bruno Delbonnel
WEST SIDE STORY—Janusz Kaminski

SCORE

★ **DUNE—Hans Zimmer**
DON'T LOOK UP—Nicholas Britell
ENCANTO—Germaine Franco
PARALLEL MOTHERS—Alberto Iglesias
THE POWER OF THE DOG—Jonny Greenwood

SONG

★ **NO TIME TO DIE *from* No Time to Die**
BE ALIVE *from* King Richard
DOS ORUGUITAS *from* Encanto
DOWN TO JOY *from* Belfast
SOMEHOW YOU DO *from* Four Good Days

ORIGINAL SCREENPLAY

★ **BELFAST**
DON'T LOOK UP
KING RICHARD
LICORICE PIZZA
THE WORST PERSON IN THE WORLD

ADAPTED SCREENPLAY

★ **CODA**
DRIVE MY CAR
DUNE
THE LOST DAUGHTER
THE POWER OF THE DOG

VISUAL EFFECTS

★ **DUNE**
FREE GUY
NO TIME TO DIE
SHANG-CHI AND THE LEGEND OF THE TEN RINGS
SPIDER-MAN: NO WAY HOME

PRODUCTION DESIGN

★ **DUNE**
NIGHTMARE ALLEY
THE POWER OF THE DOG
THE TRAGEDY OF MACBETH
WEST SIDE STORY

DOCUMENTARY

★ **SUMMER OF SOUL (...OR, WHEN THE REVOLUTION COULD NOT BE TELEVISED)**
ASCENSION
ATTICA
FLEE
WRITING WITH FIRE

ANIMATED FILM

★ **ENCANTO**
FLEE
LUCA
THE MITCHELLS VS. THE MACHINES
RAYA AND THE LAST DRAGON

BEST FOREIGN LANGUAGE FILM

The first award was presented in 1948. Until 1957 the winners were chosen without a list of nominations.

In 2020 the category was renamed
BEST INTERNATIONAL FILM

1948   ★   **SHOE-SHINE—Italy**

1949   ★   **MONSIEUR VINCENT—France**

1950   ★   **THE BICYCLE THIEF—Italy**

1951   ★   **THE WALLS OF MALAPAGA—France/Italy**

1952   ★   **RASHOMON—Japan**

1953   ★   **FORBIDDEN GAMES—France**

1954   (no award given)

1955   ★   **GATE OF HELL—Japan**

1956   ★   **SAMURAI: THE LEGEND OF MUSASHI—Japan**

1957   ★   **LA STRADA—Italy**
THE CAPTAIN OF KOPENICK—Germany
GERVAISE—France
HARP OF BURMA—Japan
QIVITOQ—Denmark

1958   ★   **NIGHTS OF CABIRIA—Italy**
THE DEVIL STRIKES AT NIGHT—Germany
GATES OF PARIS—France
MOTHER INDIA—India
NINE LIVES—Norway

1959   ★   **MON ONCLE—France**
ARMS AND THE MAN—Germany
LA VENGANZA—Spain
THE ROAD A YEAR LONG—Yugoslavia
THE USUAL UNIDENTIFIED THIEVES—Italy

1960   ★   **BLACK ORPHEUS—France**
THE BRIDGE—Germany
THE GREAT WAR—Italy
PAW—Denmark
THE VILLAGE ON THE RIVER—Netherlands

1961   ★   **THE VIRGIN SPRING—Sweden**
KAPÒ—Italy
LA VÉRITÉ—France `
MACARIO—Mexico
THE NINTH CIRCLE—Yugoslavia

1971 ★ **INVESTIGATION OF A CITIZEN ABOVE SUSPICION—Italy**
FIRST LOVE—Switzerland
HOA-BINH—France
PAIX SUR LES CHAMPS—Belgium
TRISTANA—Spain

1972 ★ **THE GARDEN OF THE FINZI CONTINIS —Italy**
DODES'KA-DEN—Japan
THE EMIGRANTS—Sweden
THE POLICEMAN—Israel
TCHAIKOVSKY—Soviet Union

1973 ★ **THE DISCREET CHARM OF THE BOURGEOISIE —France**
THE DAWNS HERE ARE QUIET—Soviet Union
I LOVE YOU ROSA—Israel
MY DEAREST SEÑORITA—Spain
THE NEW LAND—Sweden

1974 ★ **DAY FOR NIGHT—France**
THE HOUSE ON CHELOUCHE STREET—Israel
L'INVITATION—Switzerland
THE PEDESTRIAN—Germany
TURKISH DELIGHT--Netherlands

1975 ★ **AMARCORD—Italy**
CAT'S PLAY—Hungary
THE DELUGE—Poland
LACOMBE, LUCIAN—France
THE TRUCE—Argentina

1976 ★ **DERSU UZALA—Soviet Union**
LETTERS FROM MARUSIA—Mexico
THE PROMISED LAND—Poland
SANDAKAN NO. 8—Japan
SCENT OF A WOMAN—Italy

1977 ★ **BLACK AND WHITE IN COLOR—Ivory Coast**
COUSIN, COUSINE—France
JACOB THE LIAR—Germany
NIGHTS AND DAYS—Poland
SEVEN BEAUTIES—Italy

1978 ★ **MADAME ROSA—France**
IPHIGENIA—Greece
OPERATION THUNDERBOLT—Israel
A SPECIAL DAY—Italy
THAT OBSCURE OBJECT OF DESIRE—Spain

1979 ★ **GET OUT YOUR HANDKERCHIEFS—France**
THE GLASS CELL—Germany
HUNGARIANS—Hungary
VIVA ITALIA!—Italy
WHITE BIM BLACK EAR—Soviet Union

1980 ★ **THE TIN DRUM—Germany**
THE MAIDS OF WILKO—Poland
MAMA TURNS A HUNDRED—Spain
A SIMPLE STORY—France
TO FORGET VENICE—Italy

1981 ★ **MOSCOW DOES NOT BELIEVE IN TEARS—Soviet Union**
CONFIDENCE--Hungary
KAGEMUSHA (The Shadow Warrior)—Japan
THE LAST METRO—France
THE NEST—Spain

1982 ★ **MEPHISTO—Hungary**
THE BOAT IS FULL—Switzerland
MAN OF IRON—Poland
MUDDY RIVER—Japan
THREE BROTHERS—Italy

1983 ★ **VOLVER A EMPEZAR (To Begin Again) —Spain**
ALSINO AND THE CONDOR—Nicaragua
COUP DE TORCHON ('Clean Slate')—France
THE FLIGHT OF THE EAGLE—Sweden
PRIVATE LIFE—Soviet Union

1984 ★ **FANNY AND ALEXANDER—Sweden**
CARMEN—Spain
ENTRE NOUS—France
JOB'S REVOLT—Hungary
LE BAL—Algeria

1985 ★ **DANGEROUS MOVES—Switzerland**
BEYOND THE WALLS—Israel
CAMILA—Argentina
DOUBLE FEATURE—Spain
WARTIME ROMANCE—Soviet Union

1986 ★ **THE OFFICIAL STORY—Argentina**
ANGRY HARVEST—Germany
COLONEL REDL—Hungary
THREE MEN AND A CRADLE—France
WHEN FATHER WAS AWAY ON BUSINESS
—Yugoslavia

1987 ★ **THE ASSAULT—Netherlands**
BETTY BLUE—France
THE DECLINE OF THE AMERICAN EMPIRE
—Canada
MY SWEET LITTLE VILLAGE—Czechoslovakia
'38'—Austria

1988 ★ **BABETT'S FEAST—Denmark**
AU REVOIR ENFANTS (Goodbye, Children)
—France
COURSE COMPLETED—Spain
THE FAMILY—Italy
PATHFINDER—Norway

1989 ★ **PELLE THE CONQUEROR--Denmark**
HANUSSEN—Hungary
THE MUSIC TEACHER—Belgium
SALAAM BOMBAY!—India
WOMAN ON THE VERGE OF A NERVOUS BREAK-
DOWN—Spain

1990 ★ **CINEMA PARADISO—Italy**
CAMILLE CLAUDEL—France
JESUS OF MONTREAL—Canada
WALTZING REGITZE—Denmark
WHAT HAPPENED TO SANTIAGO
—Puerto Rico

1991 ★ **JOURNEY OF HOPE—Switzerland**
CYRANO DE BERGERAC—France
JU DOU—China
THE NASTY GIRL—Germany
OPEN DOORS—Italy

1992 ★ **MEDITERRANEO—Italy**
CHILDREN OF NATURE—Iceland
THE ELEMENTARY SCHOOL—Czechoslovakia
THE OX—Sweden
RAISE THE RED LANTERN—Hong Kong

1993 ★ **INDOCHINE—France**
CLOSE TO EDEN—Russia
DAENS—Belgium
A PLACE IN THE WORLD—Uruguay
(disqualified)
SCHTONK!—Germany

1994 ★ **BELLE ÉPOQUE—Spain**
FAREWELL MY CONCUBINE—Hong Kong
HEDD WYN—United Kingdom
THE SCENT OF GREEN PAPAYA—Vietnam
THE WEDDING BANQUET—Taiwan

1995 ★ **BURNT BY THE SUN—Russia**
BEFORE THE RAIN—Macedonia
EAT DRINK MAN WOMAN—Taiwan
FARINELLI: Il CASTRATO—Belgium
STRAWBERRY AND CHOCOLATE—Cuba

1996 ★ **ANTONIA'S LINE—Netherlands**
ALL THINGS FAIR—Sweden
DUST OF LIFE—Algeria
O QUANTRILLO—Brazil
THE STAR MAKER—Italy

1997 ★ **KOLYA—Czech Republic**
A CHEF IN LOVE—Georgia
THE OTHER SIDE OF SUNDAY—Norway
PRISONER OF THE MOUNTAINS—Russia
RIDICULE—France

1998 ★ **CHARACTER—Netherlands**
BEYOND SILENCE—Germany
FOUR DAYS IN SEPTEMBER—Brazil
SECRETS OF THE HEART—Spain
THE THIEF—Russia

1999 ★ **LIFE IS BEAUTIFUL—Italy**
CENTRAL STATION—Brazil
CHILDREN OF HEAVEN—Iran
THE GRANDFATHER—Spain
TANGO—Argentina

2000 ★ **ALL ABOUT MY MOTHER—Spain**
HIMALAYA—Nepal
EAST-WEST—France
SOLOMON AND GAENOR—United Kingdom
UNDER THE SUN—Sweden

2001 ★ **CROUCHING TIGER, HIDDEN DRAGON**
—Taiwan
AMORES PERROS—Mexico
DIVIDED WE FALL—Czech Republic
EVERYBODY'S FAMOUS—Belgium
THE TASTE OF OTHERS—France

2002 ★ **NO MAN'S LAND—Bosnia & Herzegovina**
AMÉLIE—France
ELLING—Norway
LAGAAN—India
SON OF THE BRIDE—Argentina

2003 ★ **NOWHERE IN AFRICA—Germany**
THE CRIME OF FATHER AMARO—Mexico
HERO—China
THE MAN WITHOUT A PAST—Finland
ZUS & ZO—Netherlands

2004 ★ **THE BARBARIAN INVASIONS—Canada**
EVIL—Sweden
THE TWILIGHT SAMURAI—Japan
TWIN SISTERS—Netherlands
ŽELARY—Czech Republic

2005 ★ **THE SEA INSIDE—Spain**
AS IT IS IN HEAVEN—Sweden
THE CHORUS—France
DOWNFALL—Germany
YESTERDAY—South Africa

2006 ★ **TSOTSI—South Africa**
DON'T TELL—Italy
JOYEUX NOËL—France
PARADISE NOW—Palestine
SOPHIE SCOLL – THE FINAL DAYS
 —Germany

2007 ★ **THE LIVES OF OTHERS—Germany**
AFTER THE WEDDING—Denmark
DAYS OF GLORY—Algeria
PAN'S LABYRINTH—Mexico
WATER—Canada

2008 ★ **THE COUNTERFEITERS—Austria**
12—Russia
BEAUFORT—Israel
KATYŃ—Poland
MONGOL—Kazakhstan

2009 ★ **DEPARTURES—Japan**
THE BAADER MEINHOF COMPLEX
 —Germany
THE CLASS—France
REVANCHE—Austria
WALTZ WITH BASHIR—Israel

2010 ★ **THE SECRET IN THEIR EYES—Argentina**
AJAMI—Israel
THE MILK OF SORROW—Peru
A PROPHET—France
THE WHITE ROOM—Germany

2011 ★ **IN A BETTER WORLD—Denmark**
BIUTIFUL—Mexico
DOGTOOTH—Greece
INCENDIES—Canada
OUTSIDE THE LAW—Algeria

2012 ★ **A SEPARATION—Iran**
BULLHEAD—Belgium
FOOTNOTE—Israel
IN DARKNESS—Poland
MONSIEUR LAZHAR—Canada

2013 ★ **AMOUR—Austria**
KON-TIKI—Norway
NO—Chile
A ROYAL AFFAIR—Denmark
WAR WITCH—Canada

2014 ★ **THE GREAT BEAUTY—Italy**
THE BROKEN CIRCLE BREAKDOWN
—Belgium
THE HUNT—Denmark
THE MISSING PICTURE—Cambodia
OMAR—Palestine

2015 ★ **IDA—Poland**
LEVIATHAN—Russia
TANGERINES—Estonia
WILD TALES—Argentina
TIMBUKTU—Mauritania

2016 ★ **SON OF SAUL—Hungary**
EMBRACE OF THE SERPENT—Colombia
MUSTANG—France
THEEB—Jordan
A WAR—Denmark

2017 ★ **THE SALESMAN—Iran**
LAND OF MINE—Denmark
A MAN CALLED OVE—Sweden
TANNA—Australia
TONI ERDMANN—Germany

2018 ★ **A FANTASTIC WOMAN—Chile**
THE INSULT—Lebanon
LOVELESS—Russia
ON BODY AND SOUL—Hungary
THE SQUARE—Sweden

2019 ★ **ROMA—Mexico**
CAPERNAUM—Lebanon
COLD WAR—Poland
NEVER LOOK AWAY—Germany
SHOPLIFTERS—Japan

2020 ★ **PARASITE—South Korea**
CORPUS CHRISTI—Poland
HONEYLAND—North Macedonia
LES MISÉRABLES—France
PAIN AND GLORY—Spain

2021 ★ **ANOTHER ROUND—Denmark**
BETTER DAYS—Hong Kong
COLLECTIVE—Romania
THE MAN WHO SOLD HIS SKIN—Tunisia
QUO VADIS, AIDA?—Bosnia & Herzegovina

2022 ★ **DRIVE MY CAR—Japan**
FLEE—Denmark
THE HAND OF GOD—Italy
LUNANA: A YAK IN THE CLASSROOM—Bhutan
THE WORST PERSON IN THE WORLD—Norway

Made in the USA
Las Vegas, NV
22 May 2022

49233375R00115